Dreaming Yourself Awake

DREAMING YOURSELF AWAKE

Lucid Dreaming and Tibetan Dream Yoga for Insight and Transformation

B. ALAN WALLACE
Edited by Brian Hodel

SHAMBHALA · *Boston & London* · 2012

Shambhala Publications, Inc.
Horticultural Hall
300 Massachusetts Avenue
Boston, Massachusetts 02115
www.shambhala.com

9 8 7 6 5 4 3 2 1

First Edition
Printed in the United States of America

⊗This edition is printed on acid-free paper that meets
the American National Standards Institute z39.48 Standard.
♻This book is printed on 30% postconsumer recycled paper.
For more information please visit www.shambhala.com.

Distributed in the United States by Random House, Inc.,
and in Canada by Random House of Canada Ltd

Designed by James D. Skatges

LIBRARY OF CONGRESS CATALOGING-IN-PUBLICATION DATA

Wallace, B. Alan.
Dreaming yourself awake: lucid dreaming and Tibetan dream yoga
for insight and transformation / B. Alan Wallace; edited by Brian Hodel.
—First edition.
Pages   cm
Includes bibliographical references and index.
ISBN 978-1-59030-957-5 (pbk.: alk. paper)
1. Lucid dreams. 2. Yoga—Tantric Buddhism. I. Hodel, Brian, editor. II. Title.
BF1099.L82W35 2012
154.6'3—dc23
2011046575

Contents

Introduction   ix

PART ONE: Lucid Dreaming

1. Meditative Quiescence: Laying the Groundwork
   for Lucidity   1
2. The Theory of Lucid Dreaming   19
3. The Practice of Lucid Dreaming   35
4. Proficiency in Lucid Dreaming   53

PART TWO: Dream Yoga

5. The Universe of Dream Yoga   67
6. The Daytime Practices of Dream Yoga   79
7. Nighttime Dream Yoga   95

PART THREE: Bringing It All Together

8. Putting Your Dreams to Work   115
9. Individualized Practice and Infrequently
   Asked Questions   123
10. Dreaming Yourself Awake: A Wider Perspective   135

Notes   151

Glossary   159

Selected Bibliography   165

Index   167

Dreaming Yourself Awake

Introduction

In all the great spiritual traditions where meditation plays an important role, the watchword is "Awaken!" This call is echoed in the Western science of psychology. The implication is that throughout our lives we've been asleep—in essence, dreaming. Of course if we sleepwalk through life we will invariably stub our toes on unseen realities. Given life's uncertainties, we need to be as awake as possible to its opportunities and dangers. *Dreaming Yourself Awake* is directed as much to our awakening from life-as-a-dream as it is to our becoming lucidly aware as we dream at night. Both situations, and our awakening within them, are intimately connected. Such an awakening brings with it the clarity and freedom that form the basis for genuine happiness.

How are spiritual awakening and lucid dreaming connected? In both cases you are poignantly aware of the unfolding of your experiences in the present moment. You are not carried away by distractive thoughts and emotions. You can observe their appearance, continuity, transformation, and fading with perfect clarity. Like a chess grand master, your mind is fully focused— sure and unclouded. Such clarity is a gateway to inner freedom. Awake to the potential of every situation, you become the master of your destiny. Dream practice can heighten creativity, solve problems, heal emotions, or provide scintillating inner theater— the ultimate in entertainment. It can also be a valuable aid to the attainment of spiritual awakening.

What is it like to be lucidly aware that you are dreaming? The seventeenth-century English philosopher and physician Sir Thomas Browne, who could witness and control his dreams like a movie director, said, "In one dream I can compose a whole Comedy, behold the action, apprehend the jests and laugh my self awake. . . ." Another seventeenth-century Englishman, Samuel Pepys, described the erotic potential of lucid dreaming: "I had my Lady Castlemayne in my arms and was admitted to use all the dalliance I desired with her, and then dreamt that this could not be awake, but that it was only a dream." The anthropologist-shaman and best-selling author Carlos Casteneda was instructed by his teacher to look at his hands while dreaming. When he first accomplished this he found himself in a surreal and forbidding landscape. Casteneda claimed he mastered the "art of dreaming" to the point that he could visit other worlds.

Dreaming Yourself Awake integrates the two most effective approaches to dream practice—*lucid dreaming*, as developed and enhanced by the science of psychology, and the *dream yoga* of Tibetan Buddhism. Together they will bring you to a life-changing awakening.

Lucid Dreaming

Lucid dreaming is simply being conscious that you are dreaming. Many people, especially in childhood, have had lucid dreams and have described them. Often in lucid dreaming there is a sense of exhilaration on discovering you are dreaming *right now*—an excitement so intense that it may cause you to awaken. If you are able to maintain both the dream and your awareness of it, there comes a great sense of freedom. Knowing that the dream images are insubstantial, you can walk through dreamed walls or escape the law of gravity, flying over vivid, imagined landscapes. With training you can shape the dream environment according to your wishes. Small things can be made large, large objects shrunk at will. The only limit is your imagination.

Once greater control has been developed you can use the dream space as a laboratory to achieve psychological insights, overcome fears, do creative work, entertain yourself, or meditate in the virtual environment of your choosing.

The science of lucid dreaming is a recently developed system of theory and practice within the field of psychology. Although he had important predecessors, Stephen LaBerge, who received his PhD in psychology from Stanford University, is the foremost exponent of lucid dreaming. In the late 1980s, LaBerge, while doing graduate research at Stanford, became the first to prove to the scientific community that one can be consciously aware while dreaming. Although many people had reported lucid dreams through the ages, psychologists assumed these were false memories—that people had actually awakened at night and in the morning mistakenly believed they had been conscious of dreaming. LaBerge is extremely gifted as a lucid dreamer and is able to have lucid dreams at will, an ability he had naturally as a child but which was lost during adolescence, then deliberately regained as a graduate student. As part of his research he devised a method of making specific eye movements while he dreamed so that his fellow researchers would know he was awake within his dreams. This method proved the existence of lucid dreaming.[1]

While at Stanford, LaBerge developed more effective means of awakening in his dreams and sustaining and vivifying them. Continued research, including interaction with interested lay persons, led to the publication of several popular books on lucid dreaming (including *Lucid Dreaming, Exploring the World of Lucid Dreaming*, and *Lucid Dreaming: A Concise Guide to Awakening in Your Dreams and in Your Life*). Due in large part to LaBerge's work, the reality of lucid dreaming has been generally acknowledged in the field of psychology. I met Stephen LaBerge in 1992 when I was a graduate student in religious studies at Stanford. My research centered on the contemplative development of attention. When Stephen and I talked about our research, we both saw immediately that our work was complementary. Beginning in the late 1990s I began collaborating with Stephen in ten-day public workshops that included training of the attention and dream practice.

DREAM YOGA

Historically, Tibetan Buddhists seem to have explored the yoga of dreaming and sleep more deeply than other contemplative traditions. *Dream yoga* is part of a spiritual tradition whose goal is the complete awakening called "enlightenment." An experience beyond our normal, rational way of understanding, full enlightenment is said to include knowledge of all reality in both breadth and depth. And it is wedded to an all-embracing compassion, a profound love for all beings. Sometimes enlightenment is described as a nondual experience of wisdom and bliss. As to the actual flavor of enlightenment, such portrayals leave us with more questions than answers, but it must be an awesome achievement.

In the Tibetan Buddhist tradition—the style of contemplative spirituality with which I am most familiar—dream yoga comprises a set of advanced spiritual practices that act as a powerful aid to awakening from *samsara*. Samsara may be briefly described as a dreamlike experience of life after life, propelled by ignorance. This, according to Buddhism (and other spiritual traditions), is our normal modus operandi. Ignorance and the distorted views woven from it are, for Buddhism, the source of all suffering. True and ultimate happiness, on the other hand, results from the elimination of ignorance, from awakening from the dream of samsara. A buddha, an enlightened one, literally means "one who is awake."

The practices of dream yoga are based upon a three-tiered theory of consciousness. According to this view, the most coarse and superficial level of consciousness is what we in the West call the *psyche*. The psyche comprises the five physical senses along with conscious and unconscious mental phenomena—thoughts, feelings, sensations, and so forth. This is our ordinary, conditioned mind. The psyche emanates from a deeper, intermediate level, the *substrate consciousness*. This is described as a subtle mind stream containing latent habits, tendencies, and attitudes tracing back to previous lifetimes. The deepest and most fundamental layer, *primordial consciousness*—encompassing both the psyche and the substrate consciousness—is an ultimate level of pure wisdom where the "inner" (mind) and "outer" (phenomenal world) are nondual. The realization of primordial consciousness is the gateway to full enlightenment.

Dream yoga seeks to gradually penetrate to primordial consciousness by way of realizing that everything, oneself included, emerges from and is of the nature of this primordial, enlightened ground. The specific practices of dream yoga enable one to explore and deeply understand the nature and origin of the mental phenomena of the psyche, to penetrate to its source—the substrate consciousness, or ground of the ordinary mind—and finally to recognize and dwell in primordial consciousness. Although it initiates this process during sleep and dreams, dream yoga involves practices employed during the daytime and aims to awaken our entire life—day and night—from the sleep of *samsara*.

My first encounter with dream yoga came in 1978, when I acted as a translator for Westerners attending teachings on dream yoga by Zong Rinpoche, an eminent Tibetan lama. He explained that dream yoga is one of a group of advanced practices called the Six Yogas of Naropa and that it requires a strong foundation in meditation. Following that advice, I engaged in foundational practices before attempting dream yoga. In 1990 I received dream yoga instruction from another revered Tibetan teacher, Gyatrul Rinpoche. Two years later a friend requested that I teach him dream yoga. I asked Gyatrul Rinpoche if I should teach it, and he gave me his permission. Over the years that I have practiced and taught dream yoga, my sense of reverence and respect for this practice has only grown. This is one of the core traditions of Tibetan Buddhism, and it has enormous implications for both our understanding of reality and our spiritual advancement.

BALANCING DREAM YOGA AND LUCID DREAMING

It has been my experience as both a practitioner and teacher of dream yoga and lucid dreaming that the two complement one another. That will be the approach taken in this book. Perhaps the most important key to developing the skills of lucid dreaming, as well as for reaching a plateau where the more advanced techniques of dream yoga can be incorporated, is *shamatha,* or meditative quiescence. Comprised of a superb range of methods for training the attention, shamatha is not a uniquely Buddhist practice. It is found in a wide variety of contemplative traditions and does not require adherence to any religious or philosophical creed. Moreover, it is extremely beneficial for both the body and the mind, providing relaxation, relief from stress, and healing, along with the sharpening of attentional skills.

With shamatha, the basic idea is to increase one's relaxed concentration to a point where one can easily sustain the attention on a chosen object. Concentration on the inflow and outflow of the breath—a method favored by the Buddha—is one such technique. One can also concentrate on a real or imagined visual image, bodily sensations, mental phenomena, or awareness itself. Once having attained a degree of stability in shamatha, the skills required for successful lucid dreaming and dream yoga come much more easily.

INDIVIDUALIZED PRACTICE

Finally, it is important to adapt the information and techniques contained in *Dreaming Yourself Awake* to your own needs and abilities. Each of us is unique. No single strategy will work well for everyone. Some of us fall asleep easily. Some don't. Some of us can remember our dreams more easily than others. Although a general sleep cycle for human beings has been discovered by psychologists, there are subtle differences among individuals. Practices and points of view that work well with one personality may be confusing and inappropriate for another. Therefore, woven into this text, I provide guidance in this area by illustrating some of these differences and proposing alternative practices—fine-tuning that will help you maximize your effectiveness as a dream yogi, a lucid dreamer. In addition to this I provide a chapter with questions and responses drawn from my retreats on lucid dreaming and dream yoga.

The good news is that whatever our limitations, awakening within dreams can be learned by anyone willing to make the effort. The key to both lucid dreaming and dream yoga—the essential ingredient that will propel us beyond the murky somnambulance of our habits—is motivation. If we become inspired to practice and committed to this inner exploration, we will succeed.

PART ONE

Lucid Dreaming

1

Meditative Quiescence

Laying the Groundwork for Lucidity

WHAT ESSENTIAL ELEMENT distinguishes a lucid dream from an ordinary dream? In a lucid dream you are aware, in real time, of the nature of the reality you are experiencing. You know that you are dreaming. You know that your body is lying in bed, asleep, even as you participate in dream episodes that range from the ordinary to the utterly fantastic. You know that all of the phenomena of your dream—the scenery and participants—are the creations of your own mind. Whereas in a nonlucid dream you take everything, no matter how bizarre it may seem, at face value—never suspecting you are asleep—in a lucid dream you know, then and there, that it's just a dream.

Ordinarily our dreams are characterized by a lack of stability. Our attention is pulled hither and yon by the contents of our dreams and our habitual reactions to these events. Shamatha is a practice that stabilizes our attention. Stability of attention is a crucial step to freedom—the freedom to transcend normal dream consciousness and recognize we are dreaming, then to maintain that lucidity, and to transform our dreams into a laboratory where we can carefully explore the mind. By gradually learning to focus our attention, confusion is replaced by an ongoing coherence—we develop command over the dream environment. Although in shamatha we are developing concentration, it is achieved not by force but through deep relaxation. This is not the stressful and ultimately exhausting concentration of the fighter pilot, who, after a few hours of exceedingly complex, skillful, and demanding maneuvers, must have at least twenty-four hours of downtime to recuperate. In shamatha the mind's distractions are stilled so that one's attention can eventually rest comfortably and effortlessly on a chosen object for hours on end.[1] That stability is an ideal platform for developing the skills of lucid dreaming and dream yoga.

The techniques leading to successful dream practice include prospective memory (preparing to remember something in a future dream), retrospective memory (remembering sequences of dream events from the past), remembering cues that alert one to the dream state, and steady, relaxed concentration on visual images. Since our ordinary states of consciousness are dominated by varying degrees of agitation and dullness, we presently lack the clarity and stability needed to make effective use of such techniques. In contrast, the relaxed, stable, and vivid mind that has been trained in shamatha is well suited to these tasks.

Let me illustrate: Maneuvering successfully in the realm of sleep—which includes the process of falling asleep, dreamless sleep, dreams, waking and returning to sleep, and remembering dreams on waking—requires greater clarity than our usual nocturnal grogginess provides. Ordinary sleep is dominated by forgetfulness.[2] Research has shown that most of us awaken and then quickly return to sleep a number of times during the night. Few notice this habit. However, these spontaneous awakenings provide one of the most useful opportunities for entering into lucid dreams. We may learn that deliberately reentering a dream after one of these intervals can lead to a lucid dream, but if we don't *remember* to do so, we will continually miss these opportunities. The clarity and stability of a mind trained in shamatha is a reliable basis for remembering to take these opportunities.

The same holds for another technique we will learn later: using typical dream events (called dream signs) to remind us while asleep that we are experiencing a dream. Over time, we can compile a list of events that occur regularly in our dreams. We may, for instance, repeatedly find ourselves in a specific location, or encounter a certain situation or the same people or objects. If we have the mental clarity to remember the importance of these signs when they appear in our dreams, that can prompt us to awaken within them. Shamatha training significantly increases the chances of this happening, whereas lacking this training, in our normal dream consciousness we are more likely to either miss these cues completely or have only a vague sensation that they are supposed to have some meaning or application.

Shamatha training is not exclusive to Buddhism. It is found in contemplative Christianity, Hinduism, Sufism, Taoism, and elsewhere. I believe, however, that Buddhism has produced a well-elaborated and broad-based shamatha program that is especially suitable for dream practice. The version I will present here draws on a tradition that makes use of three specific techniques within a framework of ten successive stages. First I will give a brief presentation of the theory of this Buddhist version of shamatha and then an overview of the more practical adaptations of this theory that we can make use of to develop skill in lucid dreaming and dream yoga.

SHAMATHA IN THEORY

The overall framework for shamatha training presented here is drawn from *Stages of Meditation*, by the eighth-century Indian Buddhist contemplative Kamalashila. There are ten stages, beginning with the coarsest of attentional states and leading up to the most subtle—the achievement of shamatha itself. With the achievement of shamatha, the practitioner will be able to concentrate effortlessly on a chosen object continuously for at least four hours. The achievement of shamatha is a rarity these days, even among dedicated contemplatives. There are two major reasons for this: In the rush to enter into and complete the "higher" practices and realizations, shamatha—even though it has been considered a requirement for such achievements—has been de-emphasized in many contemporary contemplative traditions. Second, unless one already has an extremely relaxed and balanced mind, full achievement of shamatha may require many months or even a couple of years of concentrated solitary practice. At one time, in calm, pastoral societies such as Tibet's, well-balanced minds were more common, making the achievement of shamatha possible in a shorter time span. But in today's speedy and agitated global civilization, such minds are exceedingly rare.

Although training in shamatha is not absolutely required for successful dream practice, I highly recommend it. At a minimum, the achievement of the first two of the ten stages listed below would greatly improve one's attentional stability, not only in this practice but for just about any endeavor. Accomplishing the more advanced stages, not to mention achieving shamatha itself, will make dream practice relatively quick and easy.

THE TEN STAGES IN THE DEVELOPMENT OF SHAMATHA (VERY BRIEFLY DESCRIBED):

1. *Directed Attention*—One develops the ability to focus on a chosen object.
2. *Continuous Attention*—One can maintain continuous attention on the object for up to a minute.
3. *Resurgent Attention*—One recovers swiftly when distracted from the object.
4. *Close Attention*—The object of attention is no longer completely forgotten.
5. *Tamed Attention*—One takes satisfaction in samadhi or "single-pointed concentration."

6. *Pacified Attention*—There is no longer resistance to attentional training.

7. *Fully Pacified Attention*—Attachment, melancholy, and lethargy are pacified.

8. *Single-Pointed Attention*—Samadhi is sustained without excitation or laxity.

9. *Attentional Balance*—Flawless, effortlessly sustained samadhi.

10. *Shamatha*—One can effortlessly maintain concentration on an object for at least four hours; this is accompanied by greatly increased mental and physical pliancy and other positive side effects.[3]

The main metaphor applied to these ten successive stages is the relative turbulence of a river. In the beginning, thoughts, emotions, images, and so forth course through the mind with the power of a cascading waterfall. In later stages, these mental phenomena appear with diminished force and frequency—more like a broad, calm river—until they are finally pacified completely as in a placid sea.

THREE SEQUENTIAL PRACTICES ON THE PATH OF SHAMATHA

I have found these three practices to be the most effective ones for modern people engaged in shamatha training. The first is *mindfulness of breathing*. Here one develops one's attention by observing the inhalations and exhalations, passively witnessing the tactile sensations throughout the body associated with natural breathing. The experience of the breath provides an excellent grounding, allowing physical and mental relaxation to become the basis of the practice from the very beginning. For those committed to the full shamatha training described above, I recommend that mindfulness of breathing be practiced in stages one through four. For the next three stages—five through seven—I recommend *settling the mind in the natural state*. In this practice, attention to mental phenomena replaces focus on the breath. One observes all appearing mental events— thoughts, mental images, and emotions—neutrally, objectively, without any involvement. These events—which usually draw us in—are allowed to pass before the window of the mind like clouds blown across the sky. From stage eight onward one practices *shamatha without a sign*, also called *awareness of awareness*. Previously we have been focusing on an object, that is, a *sign*. Here attention is placed on awareness itself. Whereas the breath and mental phenomena are objects identified within a conceptual framework—awareness focused on an object other than itself—here awareness simply rests within itself, luminous and cognizant.

Settling the mind in its natural state and awareness of awareness, along with other shamatha-related meditation techniques, are extremely useful for dream practice whether or not the student intends to go on to the more refined, later stages of shamatha training. I will introduce these techniques at appropriate junctures in subsequent chapters.

The instructions given in this chapter, if followed diligently, will allow the meditator to accomplish the first three stages of shamatha training. If one is inspired to go further, practice in long, solitary retreats is usually necessary. For a detailed explanation of the entire path of shamatha, see my book *The Attention Revolution*.[4]

SHAMATHA IN PRACTICE

Session One: Relaxing

Here we provide a basic meditation sequence for mindfulness of the tactile sensations of the body, which promotes relaxation— the key ingredient in shamatha practice—and is also a useful prelude for getting a good night's sleep, without which success-ful dream practice is difficult if not impossible. We will begin this and future sessions by *settling the body in its natural state.* Then, cultivating a quality of quiet, mindful presence, we will allow awareness to permeate the field of tactile sensations—those sensations arising on both the interior and the periphery of the body.

Once you have found a **comfortable posture,** do your best to remain still, apart from the movement of the breath. If sitting (on a chair or cross-legged on the floor), see that your spine is straight and your sternum uplifted just enough so that there is no pressure on your abdomen that would prevent it from ex-panding freely as you breathe in. Keep your abdominal muscles loose, feeling your belly expand with each inhalation. Wherever you find tension or tightness in the body, breathe into that area and, especially when you breathe out, release the muscular ten-sion. Pay particular attention to the muscles of the face—the jaw, the eyes. Round off this initial settling of the body by taking **three slow, deep, luxurious breaths,** breathing through the nostrils, down into the belly, expanding the diaphragm, and fi-nally breathing into the chest, breathing in almost to full capac-ity and then releasing the breath effortlessly, mindfully attentive to the sensations correlated with the breath as they manifest throughout the entire body.

Next, **settle your respiration in its natural rhythm,** noting how easy it is to influence the breath with your preferences. To the best of your ability, withdraw your control and allow the respiration to flow of its own accord, with no intervention, as effortlessly as possible.

When we begin learning meditation, we quickly discover just how agitated and cluttered our minds are. We are some-times inundated with a cascading flow of thoughts and emo-tions. Cultivate a **positive attitude,** one of patience, when you encounter these distractions. Rather than reacting by trying to clamp down and force the mind to be still, **relax and let go** of the pent-up, turbulent energy of the body-mind. Take advantage of each exhalation—a natural moment to relax and let go. With every exhalation feel a progressive sense of melting in the body, a softening, a loosening of the body. With each exhalation, as soon as you know that any involuntary thought or image has arisen, just release it without a second thought, and immediately upon release let your awareness descend quietly once again into the field of the body, simply taking note of whatever tactile sensations arise within this field, especially attending to those sensations correlated with the breath. Give yourself permission to release thoughts and to cultivate another quality of awareness that is clear, bright, intelligent, attentive, and silent.

Whenever you discover that you have become caught up in thoughts—that **your mind has been carried away**—rather than being frustrated or judgmental toward yourself, let your simple, first response be to relax more deeply, let go of the thought, and happily return your awareness to this quiet field of tactile experience. Keep the **length** of your practice session to twenty-four minutes (called, in Sanskrit, a *ghatika*, which was considered the ideal length for beginning meditation training in ancient India). Continue with the **intention** of maintaining your attention on the field of tactile sensations associated with the breath, and when you find that you have strayed, relax more deeply, abandoning distractions and returning to the body.

This practice sequence is now given in outline form so that you can dispense with the distractions caused by reading from the book as you practice. Simply take a moment to familiarize yourself with the instructions, memorize the outline, then begin.

OUTLINE OF THE PRACTICE:

- Posture: supine (*shavasana,* or corpse pose)[5] or seated
- Breathing: in a natural rhythm
- Positive attitude: cultivating relaxation

- Attention: on the field of tactile sensations
- When distracted: gently return attention to the tactile field of sensations
- Length: one ghatika (twenty-four minutes)
- Intention: to observe tactile sensations, relax and return to them when distracted

COMMENTARY

The basic technique of shamatha involves the interaction of two mental faculties: mindfulness and introspection. *Mindfulness* can be defined as continuous attention to a chosen object, which requires that one remember what the task is and not become distracted by other phenomena. *Introspection* (as the eighth-century Indian Buddhist adept Shantideva defined it) is "the repeated examination of the state of one's body and mind."[6] Therefore introspection allows for a kind of quality control, recognizing when one's attention strays and alerting mindfulness to reassert itself. One focuses one's mind using mindfulness to remember the task, and when attention strays introspection takes notice so that one can guide oneself back to the object of attention. *Remember* your intention and *check* to see that you are accomplishing it moment-by-moment.

I have a strong hunch that the manner of our breathing when we are in dreamless sleep is very restorative for the mind and body. When we are dreaming, our thoughts and emotions can interfere with our breathing. Most of us have awakened from a nightmare—perhaps one where we are being chased by something frightening—to find ourselves breathing laboriously. In dreamless sleep our compulsive thinking—hopes and fears, grasping and anticipation, and emotional activity—is dormant. Using the practice above, we can induce this restorative breathing by relaxing through the entire exhalation and then—rather than sucking in—simply allowing the inhalation to flow in passively. We gently surrender all control of the breath, unconcerned with the relative length of the inhalations and exhalations, breathing effortlessly.

The attention is allowed to be diffuse, scanning the tactile sensations associated with the breath and also the sensations emanating from the lower part of the body—the legs and lower trunk. This draws our energy and attention away from the head, grounding us and lessening interference from thoughts. At bedtime, try this practice in the supine position for a short time—five, ten, twenty minutes, or more if you like—before you go into your normal sleeping position. On the initial exhalations release first all muscular tension in the body, and once you are thoroughly relaxed physically, also release all thoughts that appear—slowly breathing out . . . out . . . out . . . —and then allow the inhalation to flow in of its own accord. Before long you will find yourself in a deep, relaxing rhythm. This will not only contribute to a good night's sleep, but is a useful prelude to lucid dreaming.

Session Two: Stabilizing the Attention

Here, after relaxing, with the attention on the tactile sensations of the body, we enter a second phase, narrowing our focus to the rise and fall of the abdomen as we breathe, promoting stability of attention.

Having settled into a comfortable posture, begin by **settling the body in its natural state,** imbued with the three qualities of relaxation, stillness, and vigilance. Having done so, round this off by taking three slow, deep breaths. Next, **settle your breathing in its natural rhythm** and then, as before, let your awareness **permeate the entire field of tactile sensations** while attending especially to those sensations correlated with the breath, wherever they arise within the field of the body. Within this field, let your awareness be diffuse.

In this first phase of mindfulness of breathing, the primary emphasis is on allowing a sense of ease, comfort, and relaxation to arise in the body and the mind. We facilitate this especially by relaxing with each exhaltion, letting go of excess muscular tension, immediately releasing any involuntary thoughts or images that arise in the mind—releasing them and immediately letting the awareness descend back into the field of tactile sensations.

A sense of ease and relaxation is indispensable for cultivating attention skills and for dream practice. But by itself it's not enough. We need to also introduce **the element of stability**—the voluntary continuity of attention. So let's step up this practice now by narrowing the focus of attention. Instead of focusing on the whole body or letting the attention rove within the body, now zero in more steadily on the tactile sensations of the rise and fall of the abdomen with each inhalation and exhalation. Narrow your focus. Continue to let the breath flow unimpeded, without constraint or effort, and with bare attention simply attend to the sensations themselves, with no conceptual overlay, no cogitation—just the sensations in the area of the abdomen corresponding to the flow of the breath.

Note the duration of each inhalation and exhalation, whether it is short or long. Continue relaxing with each exhalation, thereby **overcoming** the **agitation,** the excitation of the mind. But with each inhalation **arouse your attention,** thereby overcoming laxity and dullness. So in this way each full cycle of the breath is like a complete meditation session in itself, designed to overcome excitation and laxity and to cultivate stability and vividness. As the mind becomes calm, the attention more and more stabilized, you may find this enhances the degree of relaxation and looseness in the body and mind. At the same time, the greater the sense of relaxation in the body and mind, the easier it is to stabilize the attention. There is a synergy between these two qualities. Continue alternating relaxation and arousal of attention on the exhalations and inhalations.

And now, to help stem the flow of obsessive thinking, of being compulsively carried away by thoughts, you may find it helpful, at least occasionally, to count the breaths—to substitute many rambling thoughts for a few regular thoughts, the thoughts of counting. There are various methods; here is one: Breathe in, allowing the breath to flow in quite effortlessly, all the way to the end of the inhalation. Just before the exhalation begins, mentally, and very briefly, count "one." Then breathe out, relaxing, letting go of thoughts all the way through the exhalation. Quietly arouse your attention during the next inhalation all the way to the end, where you count mentally, very briefly, "two." So there is one count at the end of each inhalation. You may count over and over one through ten, or one through twenty-one, or you may just continue counting as you wish. Let the counting be very succinct, very brief, simply as a reminder to maintain to the best of your ability an ongoing flow of awareness of the continuous flow of sensations of the inhalation and exhalation in the area of the abdomen.

Bring the session to a close.

OUTLINE OF THE PRACTICE:

- Settle the body in its natural state
- Breathe in a natural rhythm
- Phase one: attention on the field of tactile sensations (training relaxation)
- Phase two: attention on the rise and fall of the abdomen (training stability)
- Alternate overcoming agitation (on exhalation) and arousing attention (inhalation)
- Count the breaths
- Length: one ghatika (twenty-four minutes)
- Intention: training in stability

COMMENTARY

Although the technique seems simple and straightforward, the mind that we are training—conditioned by our life experiences and cultural background—is not. The first shock beginners usually encounter is the sheer volume of mental "noise" that clutters awareness when one begins to meditate. Although it may appear that the practice itself has introduced these distractions, they have been there all along, taken for granted as part of the normal functioning of our minds. Soon we discover there are two major types of distraction that cause us to forget our task: *agitation* and *dullness*. For most of us, agitation is our biggest initial problem in focusing on a chosen object. We are in the habit of thinking rapidly, flitting among a variety of subjects— answering phone calls, chatting, surfing the internet, multitasking. We have developed a craving for objects and experiences that demands a lot of activity. Asking ourselves to suddenly slow down and focus on our breath is asking a lot.

When we are not agitated, we are often dull—fatigued from the fast, stressful pace of modern life. At these times, when we try to meditate, we find our focus hazy. The object of attention lacks vividness. We tune out, surfacing minutes later from daydreams or sleep. What we must seek then is a middle ground between agitation and dullness. To prepare this middle ground, from the start we foster the attitudes of relaxation, stillness, and vigilance. Relaxation and stillness counter agitation, while vigilance counteracts dullness. With these in mind, we are gradually able to experience moments of clarity—a respite from our normal mental flow of alternating agitation and dullness.

Session Three: Vividness of Attention

Here we will pass through the first two phases of attention on the tactile field of sensations of the body and attention on the rise and fall of the abdomen, and enter phase three—the development of vividness of attention.

Settle the body once again in its natural state, letting awareness permeate the whole field of the body, setting the body at ease, in stillness, in a posture of vigilance. If you find it helpful, take three slow, deep breaths to round off this initial settling of the body. **Settle your breathing in its natural rhythm,** an effortless flow. For a little while let your awareness continue to be diffuse, **filling the whole tactile field of the body,** letting your attention move at will within this field, attending to whatever sensations arise—especially those correlated with the breath. Keep the attention within the field of the body, without getting caught up in thoughts or carried away to other sensory fields. Continue relaxing and letting go with every exhalation.

We shift now to the second phase, where—as in the previous practice—we more narrowly focus the attention on the rise and fall of the abdomen, introducing the element of **stabilizing the attention,** deliberately cultivating a continuity of unwavering mindfulness that does not get caught up in thoughts or carried away to other sense fields. Engage with the continuous flow of sensation of the rise and fall of the abdomen with each inhalation and exhalation. Relax, let go of each exhalation as you did before, immediately releasing any involuntary thoughts or images. With each inhalation, arouse your attention, and to the best of your ability maintain a continuous flow of mindfulness on the tactile sensations corresponding to the inhalation and exhalation as they manifest at the abdomen. Let this be a full-time job. There is always something to do. Remain engaged. Sustain the focus. Relaxing with each exhalation, arousing your attention with each inhalation.

And finally, let's now introduce the element of **vividness.** We move into the third phase of mindfulness of breathing by elevating the focus of attention to the apertures of the nostrils or the area just above the upper lip, wherever you most distinctly discern the sensations of the breath flowing in and out. You are focusing your mental awareness on these tactile sensations of the breath, not your visual awareness. Keep the muscles of the face relaxed, the eyes soft, the forehead spacious. See that you are not directing your eyes to the tip of your nose, which will just give rise to tension, perhaps even headaches. So keep all of the face soft, relaxed, and focus just your mental awareness on

the sensations of the in- and outflow of the breath at the apertures of the nostrils. Focus your attention on the difference in
temperature between the sensations of the inhalation at the nostrils and the warmer exhalation. As your breathing becomes
quieter and more refined, this difference will become more and
more subtle, challenging you to become more vividly aware.

Out of sheer habit, involuntary thoughts are bound to come
tumbling out one after another; the mind will keep rambling
on. Again, in order to stem this involuntary flow of thoughts,
images, and memories, you may find it helpful again to count
the breaths, to break up the involuntary flow of thoughts. With
one count at the end of each inhalation, just before the exhalation begins, crystallize your attention, and then mindfully attend to the sensations of the breath throughout the whole course
of the exhalation. Even if there is a pause at the end of the exhalation, you may still detect sensations there at the apertures of
the nostrils. Continue attending to them and then to the sensations of the whole course of the inhalation, followed by a brief
count. To the best of your ability, maintain a continuous flow of
mindfulness; engage with the ongoing flow of sensations at the
apertures of the nostrils. In this way you exercise and enhance
the faculty of mindfulness.

In the practice of shamatha we **enhance and develop the faculty of mindfulness,** and also that of introspection—our ability to monitor the state of the mind, to monitor the meditative
process so that we quickly recognize when the mind has been
caught up in thoughts and carried away or when the mind is
simply slipping into dullness or laxity, perhaps on the way to
falling asleep. As soon as you recognize with your faculty of introspection that your attention has become agitated, carried
away, caught up in thoughts, let your first response be to relax
deeply, release the thought, and immediately re-engage with the
sensations of the breath. But first of all relax—loosen up.

And as soon as you recognize with your faculty of introspection that your mind is losing its clarity, falling into laxity or

dullness, let your first response in this situation be to arouse your attention and take a fresh interest in training the mind. Refocus on the sensations of the breath. In this way balance your attention, overcoming your proclivities toward an attention deficit, as in dullness, and attentional hyperactivity, as in agitation or excitation.

After twenty-four minutes, bring the session to a close.

OUTLINE OF THE PRACTICE:

• Settle the body in its natural state
• Breathe in a natural rhythm
• Attention on the tactile field of the body (phase one—relaxation)
• Attention on rise and fall of the abdomen (phase two—stability of attention)
• Attention on apertures of the nostrils (phase three—cultivating vividness of attention)
• Count your breaths
• Enhance mindfulness with introspection

COMMENTARY

The three phases we have developed to this point—relaxation, stability, and vividness—can be likened to the structure of a tree. The root of the whole practice is relaxation. The trunk is stability. Just as the roots of a tree support the trunk, so relaxation supports the stability of attention. And likewise, without the stability of the trunk, the foliage—the vividness of shamatha—is unsupported. You need all three qualities, and they should be in synergistic balance. If relaxation is too strong, you are likely to become dull and sleepy. If vividness is too bright and energetic, you may become agitated.

If you want to develop shamatha efficiently, don't pass over the initial development of relaxation. Try the supine position and delve deeply into that softness, looseness, and relaxation. Observe then how stability can emerge out of that great sense of ease. You can remain quite centered and focused without clamping down with tighter and tighter concentration. So relaxation and stability balance each other. Most people, when they have their first lucid dream, notice some anomaly, some odd object or event in their dream that catalyzes the awareness that they are dreaming. Then they become so excited that two seconds later they are awake. Stability born of relaxation will enable you to be grounded rather than overexcited, prolonging lucid dreams.

The second balancing act is between stability and vividness. Just as it is important that stability not be gained at the expense of relaxation, increased vividness must not weaken stability. Here you increase the clarity, luminosity, and brightness but without giving rise to agitation that would cause you to lose your coherence. The technique for increasing vividness is to focus your attention on a subtler object, such as the sensations of the breath in the area of the nostrils. It takes greater attention to follow these sensations than the relatively coarser movement of the abdomen during respiration. If introspection signals that your level of vividness is causing agitation, back off, relax, and increase stability. The overall strategy, then, is to allow stability to develop from relaxation and vividness to emerge from stability.

Naturally, each meditator's approach to these three shamatha techniques will vary according to the degree of attentiveness, agitation, and laxity we bring initially to the practice. These are qualities of our minds at present—the product of our mental habits and experience. By trying each of these techniques, alternating them, and so forth, you will gradually gain insight into your strengths and weaknesses and will refine your meditation routine appropriately, using the suggestions above as your guide. Later in the book, I will introduce other practices that will further refine your ability to accomplish the tasks required for lucid dreaming and dream yoga.

DEEPER POSSIBILITIES

While we are developing shamatha, experiences relating to much deeper layers of consciousness may spontaneously appear. These can be likened to shafts of light breaking through the clouds of our normally conditioned consciousness. They may manifest as precognition or remote viewing. I recall during one retreat there was a meditator who had no idea what would be served for lunch but described the lunch menu exactly. He was so surprised when he came down for lunch. His clairvoyant experience just arose spontaneously. I encountered similar instances of this faculty of precognition in some of the yogis with whom I lived in the hills above Dharamsala, India, in the 1980s, many of whom had been in strict, solitary retreat for decades. They noticed that they had prescient dreams the night before some unexpected visitor would arrive. I even had a student who, while doing shamatha meditation, had visions of receiving emails from certain people. Soon afterward, when she checked her email, her prescience was confirmed.

2

The Theory of Lucid Dreaming

THE STUDY OF LUCID DREAMING began in earnest three
decades ago within the field of sleep research, a branch of
psychology. The best-known researchers in the field include
Stephen LaBerge, Paul Tholey, Harald von Moers-Messmer, G.
Scott Sparrow, and Keith Hearne.[1] Western psychology only
accepted the validity of lucid dreaming in the late 1980s when
LaBerge proved its existence in a laboratory experiment. Previously, psychologists had taken it for granted that being asleep
and being conscious were mutually exclusive mental states, de-
spite the fact that lucid dreams are not uncommon. Although
the work of Stephen LaBerge and others has popularized lucid
dreaming to some degree among the general public, to date
research on lucid dreaming has not become a major scientific
endeavor.

The grudging acceptance afforded lucid dreaming by psychology is not surprising. The Western science of psychology is
itself only 140 years old and continues to struggle for respect
within the scientific community. Given its mainly materialistic
focus, science has always been reluctant to examine nonmaterial phenomena such as the mind. Indeed, in neuroscience especially, scientists have sought to define the mind and mental

phenomena as essentially material—as by-products of the physical brain composed of neurons, synapses, glial cells, neurotransmitters, and so on. According to this view, thoughts, emotions, and dreams are merely electrochemical events transpiring within the brain. Their content—"I feel good," "This pie is delicious," "I had a nightmare"—is irrelevant to chemists, biologists, neurologists, and others concerned with reducing the mind to its physical causes.

This attitude reveals an intolerance for uncertainty. Scientists really don't know the nature of the correlations between mental and neural events, but instead of facing this uncertainty, materialists simply decide that what can't be measured scientifically, namely mental events, is equivalent to what can be measured, namely brain activity. Earlier in the history of psychology, behaviorists took a similar approach by equating mental activity with physical behavior. In reality there is no evidence that subjective experiences are the same as their correlated brain processes or their resultant forms of behavior, so such assertions are unscientific. They are really nothing more than metaphysical speculations posing as scientific facts, which lead to illusions of knowledge that are the major obstacles in the pursuit of truth. All statements about mental events being located in the brain, attributing cognitive functions such as "knowing," "remembering," and "perceiving" to neurons, are based on the imagined equivalence of mental and neural events. This is tantamount to anthropomorphizing the brain, while dehumanizing ourselves as conscious beings.

Although recent discoveries (such as neuroplasticity—the ability of the brain to restructure itself from experience) have made significant cracks in this scientific stonewall, and there remain major problems in determining the precise relationship between mental phenomena and brain activity, modern brain science still holds tightly to its philosophical position based on materialism.

What a contrast this is to Eastern psychology and in particular to the history, theory, and practices of Buddhist dream yoga. Psychology, the study of the mind, was a central issue—perhaps *the* central issue—for Buddhism ever since Shakyamuni Buddha began teaching in India 2,500 years ago. Because according to the Buddhist viewpoint the world of *experience* is the gateway to knowledge, the idea that the mind might be a physical entity was not seriously considered. The contents and interrelationships of mental phenomena were of supreme importance to understanding both the mind and the physical universe. It would be fair to say that if ancient Buddhists had been presented with telescopes and microscopes, they would have been profoundly interested not only in the things that might be seen through them but also in the relationships among those data, the nature of the instruments, and the minds observing them.[2]

When we arrive at dream yoga, we will be studying theories and practices derived from the Six Yogas of Naropa,[3] dating from the eleventh century, as well as the presentation of dream yoga within the Six Bardos taught in the Nyingma lineage of Tibetan Buddhism.[4] Dream yoga has been passed down for a millennium within an empirically based tradition where the student follows the guidance of an experienced and knowledgeable teacher in the transformation and exploration of states of consciousness. Although scientific instruments are not used to prove the experiences of dream yoga, they are replicable and can be made public through the probing questions of the teacher and the detailed descriptions of the student. Anyone who wishes to make the effort can then experience them for themselves. This, then, is an "objective" or "scientific" approach on a par with LaBerge's proof of lucid dreaming. His experience was purely subjective—no one else could directly observe it. His ingenious method of demonstrating he was both asleep and conscious is in the same class as the empirical methods used by dream yogis to verify their subjective experiences. Just as LaBerge's proof was perfectly valid for demonstrating an activity that instruments could not measure, so too the empirical, subjective approach of the dream-yoga tradition may be evaluated scientifically—provided there is a will to do so.

If dream yoga is so effective and thoroughly tested, why should we bother with the theory and practice of the modern science of lucid dreaming? There are two reasons: First, dream yoga is an advanced technique appropriate for students who already possess relatively stable minds, and is usually taught only to those who have accomplished a certain level of other yogic training. Therefore it may be difficult for Westerners to enter into dream yoga without some preparation. Second, lucid dreaming—as a product of modern, Western culture—is part of our familiar, globally shared, scientific worldview. Having its roots in something familiar, lucid dreaming is easier for those familiar with Western culture to understand and apply. I believe lucid dreaming provides effective and accessible means for exploring dreams, is a good introduction to the whole field of dream practice (which includes dream yoga), and is a perfect complement to dream yoga. Using lucid dreaming as a starting point, we can integrate the two approaches for effective dream practice.

SLEEPING AND DREAMING—SOME BASICS

The field of sleep research has revealed four levels or substages of sleep that precede dreaming. They are called NREM 1 through 4 (NREM means non-rapid eye movement—in reference to whether the closed eyes are moving or not beneath the eyelids). NREM 1 is the transition between the waking state and sleep. Here we become progressively drowsier until we lose consciousness. This normally short period is characterized by slow eye movements and occasional experiences of hypnagogic imagery—vivid, dreamlike mental appearances. The first occurrence of NREM 2 lasts about twenty minutes. One is actually asleep with little mental activity, disengaged from one's physical surroundings. This is followed by NREM 3 and NREM 4, characterized by deeper sleep and exhibiting regular, large, slow, delta brain wave patterns. All of these are essentially dreamless stages of sleep. Blood pressure drops and breathing slows. This is also the deepest and most restorative sleep.[5]

Initially, after thirty to forty minutes of delta sleep, one enters REM sleep. This is where dreams occur. The sequence of the stages of sleep, then, is NREM 1, 2, 3, 4, REM. During REM sleep the body is immobilized in a type of muscle paralysis called *atonia*. The first period of REM sleep is short—five or ten minutes. One then repeats the entire cycle over and over in approximately ninety-minute cycles. The proportionate length of the REM periods increases throughout the night, with the total time in REM accounting for 25 percent of a night's sleep. (This regular profile is extremely useful as a basis for one technique of stimulating lucidity in dreams, described below.) The sleeper usually awakens briefly fifteen times or more during the night, though these awakenings are rarely noticed. They, too, can be used to enhance the practice of lucid dreaming. Furthermore, it has been discovered that the sense of the passage of time within lucid dreams closely approximates the sense of time in the waking state. If it seems you have dreamed for half an hour, that is probably the case.

DREAM CONSCIOUSNESS

In the words of Stephen LaBerge, "dreaming can be viewed as the special case of perception without the constraints of external sensory input. Conversely, perception can be viewed as the special case of dreaming constrained by sensory input."[6] According to that statement both states of consciousness—perception when dreaming and when awake—are very similar, with overlapping networks of correlated brain mechanisms. And both states can potentially be just as clear, just as "awake."

Another thing that makes waking consciousness similar to the dream state is the almost universally accepted notion that the qualities of the objects we perceive are "out there," in the objects themselves. The red of someone's red sweater or the yellow of a passing taxi is assumed to be an innate quality of the sweater or taxi. That assumption generally prevails both in waking consciousness and in nonlucid dreaming. But if we believe this, we are indeed dreaming. In fact, Western science since the time of Descartes has denied this seemingly intuitive assertion. The experienced qualities of external objects are not contained in the objects themselves but are as illusory and dreamlike as are the qualities of a fire-breathing dragon experienced in a nightmare. How so?

In a general sense our perception may be "constrained" by the physical objects we perceive, but the perceived qualities in those objects, such as color, brightness, texture, temperature, odor, taste, and so forth, arise from the interaction of external sensory input, brain functions, and the stream of consciousness. The notion that such qualities are inherent in objects is negated by science. For example, the sun may emit photons (which can be registered by scientific instruments), but it is our perceptual and conceptual organs that experience what we call "light." The duality of light versus dark is built into us (and other beings that perceive things in this way), but these qualities do not exist "out there" in the world. The sun, in itself, is not "bright." Nor is it "hot." It emits photons and thermal radiation that we perceive as bright and hot. The fields of biology and physics have established this as scientific fact.

It becomes a little easier to accept this uncommon notion when we think of animals such as certain deep-sea and cave-dwelling species that are blind. It would seem that for them there is no light and no dark. The same goes for humans who are blind from birth. They know of light (and dark) only from what they've been told by humans with sight. Likewise, for the deaf there is no sound or silence (though sound waves might be felt with the body). Furthermore, other creatures perceive photons, sound waves, and other sense data in ways that are sometimes radically different from ours. Just imagine the variety of odors experienced by dogs. So the qualities of the objects we perceive arise in dependence upon our minds and bodies in interaction with the environment. To believe otherwise is to live under the spell of an illusion—one that pervades both our waking and dreaming consciousness. Seen from this perspective, the effect of conditioning on our perceptions creates a dreamlike reality. Humans dream of human realities, but dogs may dream in scents, whales of underwater songs.

When we are awake we experience the world according to our conditioning. For example, we gained some of our initial experiences of gravity as toddlers when we learned to walk. We fell frequently—some "force" kept pulling us down when we lost our balance. The whole notion of balance in sitting up, standing, walking, and running involves an active interplay with gravity. So gravity—whatever that is (there are several scientific hypotheses)—is a physical constraint experienced with waking consciousness. We became conditioned to it in specific ways when we learned to move about as children. In dreams, however, it is possible to escape the law of gravity. Physical laws don't apply in the nonphysical realm of dreams, in which floating in the air and flying through space are not unusual. In lucid dream training, one of the earliest acquired skills is to fly at will. So, as Stephen LaBerge suggests above, dreams are a mode of experience not constrained by physical input from the environment.

It might be more accurate to say that dream consciousness is not as rigidly conditioned as waking consciousness. In fact, lucid dreamers sometimes have to train themselves to fly. The notion of gravity is so ingrained that it may carry over into the dream state. In that case a lucid dreamer may need to learn to fly in stages, gaining confidence that in the dream realm one won't come crashing down and injure oneself. Because one *believes* that gravity prohibits one from flying, one can't fly. Overcome that belief, and you're free of the conceptually imposed constraints of gravity. So conditioning plays an important part in the qualities perceived in both waking and dreaming consciousness. Because the sun we may perceive in a dream is purely imaginary, it does not exist ninety-three million miles from us and does not emit photons or thermal energy. Even so, we may perceive a sun in our dreams that is both bright and warm. But since there is no physical sun in our dreams constraining our perception, we may also choose to experience there a sun in the shape of a cube that emits rays of cold, green light.

That brings us to the essence of both waking and dream consciousness: they are both forms of awareness, the same awareness through which we *know*—in the broadest and most basic sense—everything we experience. And this awareness can be influenced—it is malleable and subject to conditioning. Dream yogis seek to transcend that conditioning to attain enlightenment—the direct experience of reality that is the ultimate goal of Buddhism and other contemplative disciplines. Lucid dreamers seek to use the malleability of consciousness for a variety of reasons, including spiritual realization. By exploring dream consciousness directly—by running experiments—both traditions have devised theories and practices that each of us can confirm if we invest sufficient time and energy.

STRATEGIES FOR LUCIDITY

Dullness and amnesia—which operate hand-in-hand—are the major obstacles to lucidity as we sleep. Dullness puts us in a daze that prevents us from functioning with anything like the sharpness of our daytime mentality. Amnesia keeps us from remembering while dreaming that we are asleep. As we dream, we are often involved in activities that are inconceivable from a waking perspective, assuming all the while that they are real, without ever questioning whether we are asleep or awake. The science of lucid dreaming has evolved a number of effective strategies for combating this state of torpor.

THE POWER OF MOTIVATION

One is not likely to get very far in lucid dreaming by taking a casual attitude. Many of the practices of lucid dreaming derive their effectiveness from a positive, proactive motivation based on an intense interest and desire to achieve and develop lucid dreaming. This approach is found in dream yoga as well. Apprentice dream yogis are encouraged to prep themselves with strong and repeated statements such as, "Tonight I definitely will recognize the dream state!" spoken out loud prior to sleep. Lucid dreaming uses a number of such strategies enacted both in the daytime and at bedtime to increase the chances of lucid dreaming. These have a sound basis in common reminders we use to awaken at a specific time. When necessary, many of us are able to awaken at a predetermined hour in the morning without the use of an alarm clock. If, for instance, we are traveling and forget to bring an alarm clock, and we need to catch an early flight, we can awaken through the power of a strong suggestion: "I must get up at 6 A.M.!" The same internal mechanism enables mothers to awaken spontaneously at a specific hour early in the morning to feed their babies. It has to be done, so they do it.

Another useful way to prime ourselves for lucid dreaming is to anticipate lucid dreams during our waking hours. At intervals throughout the day we imagine ourselves becoming lucid during a dream. We may imagine a recent dream and see ourselves becoming lucid—perhaps triggered by something odd or impossible that occurred in the dream. This kind of anticipation is especially effective if we do it as we are falling asleep.

These are examples of *prospective memory:* preparing to remember at a later time a suggestion made previously. In lucid dreaming, the technique is considerably refined with the use of *dream signs* derived from a *dream journal*. Keeping a journal with detailed descriptions of your dreams serves several purposes. First, in order to have something to write in your journal you must be able to remember your dreams. It has been shown that excellent dream recall is a crucial factor in developing lucid dreaming. The field of lucid dreaming has discovered several techniques for improving memories of dreaming. Since we learn in the early stages of lucid dream training that we tend to forget our dreams easily, learning to lie still on waking, and to immediately cast our attention backward to the dream from which we have emerged, will enable us to capture its details. Second, using prospective memory to enable us to remember to lie still, think back, and remember dreams is itself an introduction to a more advanced technique that can be applied both to trigger lucidity and to train within the lucid dream state.

This more advanced form of prospective memory requires that you discover personal dream signs. These are typical objects, characters, situations, and moods that appear in your dreams. Once enough material has been gathered in your dream journal, an analysis is made to discover things that repeat frequently and to categorize these phenomena. You then familiarize yourself with them, making them the target of prospective memory. If one of your dream signs is, say, the repeated appearance of a white rabbit, you train yourself with the reminder, "The next time I see a white rabbit, I will ask myself whether or not I'm dreaming."

This strategy can be further refined by attaching a *state check* to the recognition of a dream sign. There are a number of activities you can perform to check your state, to determine whether you are dreaming or awake. As mentioned previously, one often can float or fly in dreams. It also happens that in dreams printed text and digital clock numerals tend to change when you look away then return your gaze. If you read something in a dream that says "mom" on first glance, if you look away and then back it will very likely have changed to some other word, perhaps "mob" or "mop," or something completely different. Another difference between dreaming and the waking state, as mentioned previously, is gravity. In a dream, if you jump straight up, you will likely descend at a slower rate than during the waking state. Using the above example, then you would prep yourself by affirming, "The next time I see a white rabbit I will jump up in the air. If I float or descend more slowly than usual, I will know I am dreaming and become lucid." Eventually you will do just that. When you have gathered in your dream journal a number of personal dream signs verified by repeated appearances, you possess a very useful tool for awakening within your dreams. Stephen LaBerge, who developed this approach, calls it MILD—Mnemonic Induction of Lucid Dreams. The dream sign is a mnemonic device prompting a specific response through prospective memory.

As you become skilled in remembering your dreams you will begin to notice oddities or *anomalies*—things that are so bizarre that it is surprising you don't question them as you dream along, believing your dreams are real. Anomalies, ranging from flying elephants to green sunsets to the appearance of deceased relatives to nightmares inhabited by fantastic creatures, occur in most people's dreams at least from time to time, but our normal dream state, dominated by dullness and amnesia, prevents us from questioning them. In other words, there is something missing here—we lack a *critical reflective attitude*. During normal waking experience we maintain a certain degree of skepticism garnered from our life experience. We all develop our own conception of what is possible in life. If a salesman offered us a new car for ten dollars or we saw a flying elephant, most of us would immediately become skeptical, if not a bit worried about our sanity. Such phenomena would be considered very odd—the kind of thing that happens only in imagination or in dreams.

The cumulative effect of the strategies described above is to awaken our critical reflective attitude, to make us sensitive to oddities we frequently experience while dreaming that could trigger lucidity. Another training strategy that enhances this attitude is to make periodic state checks during waking hours. One may simply get in the habit of asking oneself, "Am I dreaming or not?" ten or fifteen times per day. Or one could cultivate the habit of asking such a question on specific cues, such as each time one walks through a doorway or when something bizarre or unusual occurs. Each time the question is asked one can do a state check, like jumping into the air to see if one is indeed dreaming. Training consistently in this way will eventually create a habit that will carry over into your dreams: if every time you walk through a door you ask, "Am I dreaming?" eventually when you walk through a door in a dream you will, out of habit, ask that same question, conduct a state check, and thereby trigger lucidity—"Hey! I *am* dreaming!"

The most common way we become lucid while dreaming is by experiencing something spectacularly strange that startles us into lucidity. For this reason, unpleasant dreams such as nightmares most commonly serve as such a trigger. LaBerge calls such dreams DILDs—Dream-Initiated Lucid Dreams. One variation on this is to use an alarm clock to awaken yourself periodically during the night. If your alarm awakens you from a dream, and you have trained yourself to remember your dreams upon waking (remaining motionless and reflecting back on the dream contents), you may be able to fall back into the dream consciously and continue the dream lucidly. The chances of your accomplishing this are particularly good during the last two hours of sleep—prime time for lucid dreaming. If you have the time—say, on weekends—you can extend this possibility by sleeping in an extra hour or two. You can also deliberately awaken yourself toward the end of the sleep cycle and read (particularly something related to lucid dreaming) for half an hour. You then set your resolve to dream lucidly and go back to sleep. Stephen LaBerge has calculated that this strategy increases your chances of lucid dreaming by 2,000 percent.

The approach of surfacing and then reentering sleep is called WILD—Wake-Initiated Lucid Dreams.

Another version of WILD is to follow the hypnagogic imagery that often appears as we fall asleep. These images range from partial dreamlike scenes to elaborate geometric patterns. They are very subtle and require relaxation and sensitivity to perceive, but if you can maintain gentle attention on them once you see them, you can fall asleep consciously and experience both dreams and non-REM sleep lucidly.

Training in the Dream

It is an exciting experience to have your first lucid dream—especially if it is accomplished intentionally. In fact it is so exciting, bizarre, unexpected, and energizing that you usually awaken after only a few seconds of lucid dreaming. So the next step is to develop some stability, increase your "flight time." One contributing factor that cannot be overlooked is your ability to sleep regularly. If you can't get a good night's sleep, developing stability in lucid dreaming is impossible. In the next chapter I will offer suggestions and exercises that will help you fall asleep more easily and extend your sleep time.

Techniques such as those outlined above, if practiced diligently, will eventually enable you to engage in lucid dreaming more frequently. Thereafter to extend or stabilize lucid dreams requires that you (1) keep the dream going (don't wake up or fall into dreamless sleep), and (2) maintain lucidity (don't fall into ordinary, nonlucid dreaming). Once you are able to maintain a lucid dream for more than a few seconds, you may notice the dream scenario begins to break up. The images lose their sharpness and cohesiveness. There are a number of techniques you can apply via your "dream body" to stimulate your senses and revive the integrity of dream contents. Techniques derived from meditation for creating vividness of consciousness can also be applied to your dreams to enhance their intensity. These practices will be introduced later.

The techniques used for reconstituting dreams are based on the theory that competing sense data from either the waking state or from dreamless sleep are responsible for the deterioration of lucid dreams. Following that logic, practices have been developed that focus your attention on the dream phenomena, thereby diminishing outside interference and allowing the dream to be reconstituted. By ramping up the relative vividness of the dream scenario, the power of interference is relatively diminished. Similarly, there are techniques for maintaining lucidity that range from simple reminders ("This is a dream") to the creation of story lines that will extend both the dream and your lucidity within it.

PUTTING DREAMS TO USE

Once you have established some stability in lucid dreaming, it's time to make use of this new skill. Each person will, of course, have his or her own aims and interests. For example, I recall one extremely skilled lucid dreamer who in waking life was confined to a wheelchair. Lucid dreaming was her opportunity to escape this situation and move around in ways far more varied and fulfilling than the normal activities of those of us free of physical disabilities. Not only could she have lucid dreams at will, and of course fly to any place she imagined, but she could transform her dream body into any object she chose. So here is an example of how lucid dreaming can help one compensate for physical limitations.

In lucid dreams, those attracted to extreme sports can go far beyond anything possible in ordinary life. One can also train physical skills in lucid dreams. This parallels the kind of mental training athletes employ using visual imagination to rehearse physical movements. Concert musicians have been known to train away from their instruments (for instance on airplane flights), fingering invisible pianos, violins, and so forth, while imagining or hearing mentally the music they are practicing. All of these techniques can be applied to even greater advantage in lucid dreaming because you can create the perfect virtual environments for training. If you've always wanted to play a Stradivarius, you can have one!

You can also create and program fantasies and adventures in lucid dreams. Anything you can see on television, the silver screen, in a video game, or read in a book can be done in the creative realm of lucid dreaming. You can play the lead in a self-created drama—or be all the actors. You can go backward or forward in time as if you were playing a DVD. Your imagination is the only limit as to how you can entertain yourself.

Personally, I prefer to view lucid dreaming as a laboratory for exploring the mind. If you take, say, a Western psychological viewpoint, lucid dreaming can allow you to explore your fears, neuroses, psychological obstacles, and so forth. If you are having difficulty interacting with a boss, coworker, or other acquaintance, you can conjure up that person in your dreams and rehearse your interactions. Even unfinished business with a deceased relative can be reenacted in a lucid dream because in the dream space you can bring that person (as you conceive of or remember that person) back to life. In the process of such explorations you may learn new things about yourself. A fear of heights can be worked through by re-creating threatening situations in lucid dreams. You can practice walking over tall bridges, experiencing the sense of height while simultaneously aware that it is all a dreamscape. You can jump off the bridge if you like, and you will merely float down to "earth." The possibilities for therapeutic role-playing are endless.

In dream practice there are techniques by which you can perform a variety of transformations that challenge and stretch the limits of your identity. What are the boundaries of the ego we label "I"? What would it be like to go beyond them? This is essentially a spiritual question. In many contemplative religious traditions, going beyond the dualism of "self" and "other" is a major aim. This is one of the main topics of dream yoga, which we will explore further down the road. In chapter 8 we will examine these and related activities in greater detail.

OUTLINE OF LUCID-DREAMING TECHNIQUES:

- The power of **motivation** (making positive affirmations like, "Tonight I will definitely recognize that I am dreaming!")
- **Prospective memory** (planning ahead and imagining an outcome, for example, during the day imagine becoming lucid in a dream)
- Noting **dream signs** and writing them down in a **dream journal**
- Performing **state checks** (try to fly; look at written material, turn away, and look again)
- Noticing **anomalies** ("How odd is *that*?")
- Developing a **critical reflective attitude** ("Is *this* possible?")
- Following **hypnagogic imagery**
- **MILD**—Mnemonic Induction of Lucid Dreams (performing a state check when you see a dream sign)
- **DILD**—Dream-Initiated Lucid Dreams (deliberately waking in the night and returning to an ongoing dream lucidly)
- **WILD**—Wake-Initiated Lucid Dreams (waking in the night, reading, then reentering sleep lucidly)
- **Reconstituting fading dreams** (spinning your dream body, giving it a rub-down)
- **Maintaining fading lucidity** (reminding yourself, "This is a dream," creating story lines)
- Using the **later hours** effectively (the last two hours of sleep are best for lucid dreaming; even better, on weekends you could sleep a couple of extra hours)

3

The Practice of Lucid Dreaming

NO SLEEP, NO DREAMS

It's no surprise that many of us don't sleep as well as we would like or as much sleep as we need. Whether you live in New York or Beijing, the stress and long working hours that epitomize the modern lifestyle interfere with the natural sleep pattern. Statistics from 2008 show that fifty to seventy million Americans have chronic sleep and wakefulness disorders, with twenty-nine million U.S. adults reporting they sleep less than seven hours per night.[1] Many of us must wake up early, joining the morning rush to jobs that are often a rush unto themselves. We are bombarded by worrisome news about politics, economics, and health. Social transformations often rock our relationships with friends, family, and partners. We seem to be harried from all sides. Paradoxically, to cope with all of this stress, a good night's sleep is just what the doctor ordered. Another excellent remedy for coping with the vicissitudes of life is shamatha meditation. Practicing this technique at bedtime will help you sleep longer and more soundly as well as prepare you for lucid dreaming.

Shamatha Practice to Improve Sleep

This practice has two parts: *settling the body in its natural state* and *settling the breathing in its natural rhythm* (both described previously). At bedtime, lay down in the **supine position** with your body straight, head on your pillow, arms at your sides. Rest your awareness in a purely witnessing mode, quiet and attentive, simply noting the tactile sensations arising within the field of sensations of your entire body. If you discover areas that are tight or constricted, breathe into them, and as you release the breath, let it carry away any tension. Surrender your muscles to gravity—let them melt, soften. Bring awareness to the face, the muscles around mouth and chin, and soften them. Check the muscles of your jaws and release them. Shift your attention to the forehead. Allow a sense of openness and spaciousness there. Open the area between the eyebrows, soften the eyes, and let the whole face rest in an expression as gentle and relaxed as a sleeping baby, without a care in the world.

In this way we **settle the body in its natural state,** imbued with the three qualities of relaxation, stillness, and vigilance. Round off this initial settling of the body by taking three long, deep, refreshing breaths. Breathe down into the abdomen and expand upward through the diaphragm and chest. When your lungs are almost full, release your breath and let it flow out effortlessly. Settling the body in this way is already a fine facilitator for getting a good night's sleep—but we can do more.

Now that your body is relaxed, at ease, in comfort, there should be no difficulty in your remaining perfectly still so that you can focus the continuity of your attention on the breath. In the supine position, the belly, diaphragm, and chest can move easily as you breathe. Now **settle your respiration in its natural rhythm,** whatever rhythm that may be at this moment, with no preconceived idea of how it should be. Let the breath flow as effortlessly, as unimpeded as you can. The inhalations and exhalations may be long or short; there may be pauses now and again. Observe the sensations of the breath closely but passively; relinquish all preferences. Let the body breathe of its own accord.

Allow the tightness of the body to melt away with each exhalation, and, as if it were a gust of wind blowing away dry leaves, simply **release any involuntary thoughts, mental images, or activities of the mind.** Let them go, breathe out with a sigh of relief, as if to say, "I don't have to think all of the time, sometimes it's OK to be quiet," and just be present, mindfully attentive to the tactile sensations arising throughout the body, especially those correlated with the breath. This is a time for quiescence rather than stimulation—a time simply to be present rather than active or reactive. With each exhalation, deeply let go in body and mind. Continue releasing and relaxing all the way through the exhalation, until the inhalation flows in as effortlessly and spontaneously as a wave washing up on the shore.

When you become drowsy, roll over into your normal sleeping position, and allow yourself to drift off to sleep.

OUTLINE OF THE PRACTICE:

- Posture: supine (on your back, arms flared out slightly)
- Body settled in its natural state
- Breathing settled in its natural rhythm
- Mental activity released with the breath
- Intention: to relax away all physical and mental activity and tension as preparation for a good night's sleep

Getting Started with Lucid Dreaming

The first step toward lucid dreaming is to generate interest in your dreams. If you don't have a natural curiosity about your sleeping and dreaming, think about this: should you live to the age of ninety, about thirty years—an entire third of your life—will pass in your sleep. All of those years you will spend in a semiconscious or unconscious state. It's almost like spending a third of your life in a coma. That's a pretty big chunk. Sure, we all need our sleep. But what if you could use some of that time to do a wide range of interesting, meaningful, and fulfilling activities without depriving yourself of the rest you need? If you can learn lucid dreaming and apply that skill to some of your major interests—creative endeavors, improving skills, spiritual and psychological exploration, fun and adventure—that would be like having a significant number of very meaningful years added to your life span.

Tonight, then, as you are falling asleep, develop the strong resolve to take interest in your dreams. Be very gung ho about it: "Tonight, I am going to pay attention to my dreams!" Say it over and over. The chances are high that you will go through five to seven dream cycles, so there will be plenty of material there to pay attention to. "And when I awaken, be it during the night or in the morning, I am going to do something out of the ordinary: I am going to remain still from the very moment I begin to wake up. And having achieved that through prospective memory— remembering now at bedtime to do something (to be immobile) in the future—I am then going to engage in *retrospective memory*. I am going to cast my mental glance backward within the dream from which I have emerged or to whatever dream I can remember. I am going to try to go back frame-by-frame as far as possible, to capture as much of that dream as I can."

Why remain immobile? Our memory of dreams, especially when we begin dream practice, is fleeting. When we move upon awakening, we immediately engage in a new environment with all of its sensory information. A dream that seemed riveting only seconds earlier can vanish instantly. However, if we remain still and keep our eyes closed, we are only halfway out of dreamland. The atmosphere of our dream still lingers, and this gives us a chance to recapture at least some of the story. So you must remain immobile from the instant you begin to emerge from sleep. Even if you remember this task a few seconds after you have awakened, it is already too late. You might be able to catch some of your dream, but the chances diminish the longer you wait. When trying to remember dreams it is also important to maintain a relaxed mind. If we become tense or overexcited due to high expectations, our thoughts may interfere with the images we seek to recall.

If you are unable to get very far in your task of remembering a dream, there are questions you can pose that may jog your memory. If you've picked up the tail end of a dream, ask yourself, "Where was I, and what was happening just before that? How did I get there? Why was I there? What did I want? What was I fleeing from? What was I chasing after?" Get in the habit of asking such questions when you get stuck. But remembering even a piece of your dream would be quite a bit for your first night of dream practice. If you were able to remain still upon waking, and remember why you did so, you have opened the door to the use of prospective memory in lucid dreaming. You made a date with yourself to do something in the future, and you did it. That is an important step.

Once you are able to get even a single fragment from any dream you've had during the night, write it in your dream journal. As we continue training in this way, our memory for dreams will improve. In the beginning we may operate in the following manner: "OK, I'm beginning to wake up. I will remain motionless—that's the first task. Now, what's the second? Oh yeah, try to remember what I was dreaming. What was my last thought, last image—my last experience? Maybe it was a dream image, a dream experience." So you keep casting back, fishing for material. If something doesn't come immediately, keep on trying. By doing so, eventually it will work. "Can I remember *anything* since I fell asleep last night? Any images? Any story? Any emotions? Anything at all?" If you pick up the end of a dream, concentrate on that, thinking, for example, "OK, that was a dream.

I was in Los Angeles. How did I get there? By plane? Where was I coming from? I see now, I came from Denver." Maybe those two frames are all you will get, or maybe you will be able to unpack the whole dream. But over time, prompting yourself in this way will improve your memory for dreams and you will be able to remember many dreams from a single night, in their entirety and in great detail, without having to prime the pump with questions.

A POSITIVE ATTITUDE

You may be able to keep still on awakening and remember some of your dream on your first attempt. If so, great! But it also may take you some days for this to occur. No matter how long it takes—and this advice goes for any of the stages of dream practice—*remain positive*. Learning lucid dreaming does not require special talent. But it is an unusual skill based on establishing habits that may not be a normal part of your lifestyle. Rather than becoming negative, beating up on yourself ("I'm no good at this!"), tell yourself, "I wasn't able to do it this time, but in the future it will be possible. I shall accomplish this." Keep in mind as well that taking delight in small successes is a much more effective strategy than being disappointed by big failures set up by unrealistic expectations.

It was shown in the previous chapter that there are many steps on the road to expertise in lucid dreaming. Naturally you will pass through periods when the going is easy and other times when it is more difficult. At any juncture where you are obstructed temporarily, take this advice to heart and remain positive and patient. The scientific data from lucid dream research proves conclusively that these methods work. But lucid dreaming is more of an art than a simple skill like learning to type. Each dreamer is different, so each pathway to learning lucid dreaming varies somewhat.

The Dream Journal

Before long you will be able to remember longer and longer passages from multiple dreams, if not entire dreams. From the beginning of this process, keep a notebook close by your bed and as soon as you have remembered as much dream material as you can for a given night or period of the night, write it down in as much detail as possible. I have seen people who began with zero dream recall remembering four or five dreams per night. Some participants in a three-month retreat I once led spent forty-five minutes to an hour each morning writing out all the dream material from the previous night. By the time you have gotten really good at this, perhaps in a month or two, you can stop writing. You'll then be able to remember your dreams very easily. The written material you've accumulated will be employed in the next step—identifying your dream signs.

A dream sign is something that repeats in your dreams. Therefore, the appearance of one of these recurring phenomena is a clue revealing that right now you are dreaming. The character of each person's dream signs is different. Here are some standard categories: (1) A dream sign may be a person who reappears dream after dream. (2) It may be a scenario that repeats—a conversation or an argument. (3) It may be a specific situation or environment. In the same setting you might be doing different things. (4) It may be an emotion, such as a particular emotional slant you take on a situation. (5) Anomalies or oddities are a type of dream sign. (If you were sitting at home and a raccoon walked into your living room, circled your chair three times, and then walked back out—that's possible, but *very* unlikely. It may well be an anomaly indicating that you are dreaming.) (6) Impossibilities are dream signs with an exclamation point. (If the raccoon flew into your room, sang an aria from an Italian opera, then flew back out, that would be impossible—unless you were dreaming.)

In my case one such repeated scenario is finding myself traveling—say in an airport or bus station—and I am worrying about having lost or forgotten something. This no doubt derives from my having been an avid traveler since I was a young man. Therefore in my youth I was frequently anxious that I might have lost my passport, forgotten to get a visa, forgotten one of my bags, or missed my connection. Since such situations recur in my dreams, they may be classified as dream signs. When I experience such traveler's anxiety, for me there is a good chance that I am dreaming. This is a repeated emotion associated with a specific situation. Another similar example I know of is a musician who repeatedly dreams he is performing a solo concert before a packed audience. He is playing along nicely only to discover that he is playing the wrong instrument—an instrument he has never learned. He is then overwhelmed by stage fright as he tries to keep playing and finally by embarrassment as the music falls apart. Note that dream signs may change over time. One that was hot six months ago may stop appearing, replaced by a new one.

Once you have accumulated sufficient material in your dream journal—descriptions of at least twenty dreams—you perform an analysis to determine your dream signs. Some you may have noticed already—occurrences that are in some degree *odd* or that *recur*. Look for oddities regarding *identity:* Who were you in the dream? If you were someone or something other than yourself, that's certainly odd. Likewise if your age was different—in the dream you were significantly younger or older than your present age. Was your identity changing within the dream? Did you shape-shift from a human into a cat or a car? What about odd *activities*? Were you flying, passing through walls, walking on water? What about odd and repeated *environments*? Do you frequently find yourself in the same dreamscape? Are the surroundings odd—blue plants, purple sky, red clouds, two suns? Or the environments you visit frequently in dreams might be perfectly normal, such as your workplace, your hometown, or a nearby restaurant. If some such location comes up repeatedly in your dream journal, you can look for it in your dreams.

The *people and objects* in your dreams can be signs. Have you been conversing with extraterrestrials—or with your dog (who answers back)? Are some of the people in your dreams now deceased—a relative or famous person? Do you have coffee with Frank Sinatra or John F. Kennedy? Finally there are repeated *emotions*, such as my travel anxiety from long ago. Certain situations may trigger dread or desire or disbelief in a manner that is unusual or different from your normal daytime emotional responses. Of course there are other possible categories, but these will serve to get you started.

Developing a Critical Reflective Attitude

The motive for becoming familiar with your dream signs is to trigger lucidity within your dreams. By logging a sufficient number of dreams in your journal and extracting a list of dream signs, you eventually get a useful and quite interesting picture of your dream life. The point of this—in terms of dream practice—is not to analyze your dreams in order to discover psychological patterns as is done in traditional psychoanalysis or Jungian dream work. Although you may pick up quite a lot of new information about your psyche in the process of recording your dreams, the learning in this tradition comes from the activities and insights of lucid dreaming itself. For instance, through psychoanalysis you may discover that you have a hidden fear of some object, person, or situation, and you may discover its origin, say, in a childhood trauma. In lucid dreaming you may not only discover such a hidden fear but also be able to confront that fear lucidly in your dreams—repeatedly—and overcome it. For example, you may forgive and be forgiven by placing yourself in a replica of an original situation that traumatized you or caused you embarrassment. By revisiting it, you may accept and integrate a situation that occurred years ago but is still disturbing you.

Having familiarized yourself with a number of your recurrent dream signs, the next step to jogging yourself awake in your dreams is to train again in prospective memory—do something the next time you encounter a dream sign. That something will be a *state check*. If one of your dream signs is seeing a pink elephant, you will tell yourself, "The next time I see a pink elephant, I am going to jump up in the air. If I descend slowly or fly, that will prove that I am dreaming and I will become lucid." As we saw before, such exceptions to gravity are effective state checks. Unless you are an astronaut on a mission, you will be able to do that only if you are dreaming. Therefore, become intimately familiar with your current dream signs and anticipate performing a state check when one of the signs appears.

This tactic alone may prove sufficient for triggering lucidity with enough frequency for you to become proficient in lucid dreaming. But for most of us it takes a bit more to break through the dullness and amnesia that prevent us from questioning the nature of the reality we're experiencing. The fact that the natural occurrence of lucid dreams is so infrequent shows that the fog is very thick. We need to create strong habits that encourage lucidity to combat our long-established tendency of somnolence and credulity. Therefore we establish the habit of making state checks during the daytime. By doing so we train, reinforce, and perfect our abilities in prospective memory. This method is a daytime parallel to the use of dream signs at night.

DAYTIME STATE CHECKS

To develop prospective memory, make a list of twenty-five to thirty typical activities that you perform on a daily basis. These can include simple actions like walking through a door, turning a door knob, seeing a bird or animal, noticing a car or house of a particular color, hearing music, looking at yourself in the mirror, tying your shoes. Try to have your list cover activities that involve all of your senses. Then choose four or five for each day of the week, at random. At the beginning of each day, memorize the handful of activities listed for that day, and the first time you perform that activity, you are to notice it immediately and then perform a state check. For instance, if your activity is to notice the first time you walk through a door, and your state check is to jump up in the air, that is what you will do. As a slight variation, when you catch yourself performing one of your targeted activities, you can first ask yourself, "Am I dreaming or not?" and then jump into the air.

Aside from jumping into the air, there are other reliable state checks to determine if you are dreaming or not. Research has shown that by reading something once, looking away, and looking back at the same material, the chances are 85 percent that in a dream the words will change. The same is true for digital clocks and watches. If you look at a digital timepiece in a dream, turn away, then look back, the chances are high that the numbers will have changed. You can also try pulling your nose. In a dream, doing this will often cause your nose to grow, like Pinocchio's.

By performing state checks on a daily basis, you will instill the habit of doing the same things in a dream. Walking through a doorway may not be an oddity—whether in daytime or dreaming—but it may happen frequently in your dreams. If you were to get into the habit of performing a state check each time you walked through a doorway, even of merely asking yourself, "Am I dreaming or not?" sooner or later you will do the same thing in a dream. By training in this way you will reinforce the possibility of making state checks when dream signs, oddities, anomalies, and impossibilities occur in your dreams. You notice there are two suns in the sky, you ask, "Am I dreaming or not?" and you trigger lucidity. This training, as we saw in the previous chapter, is what Stephen LaBerge calls MILD— Mnemonic Induction of Lucid Dreams.

The result, over time, will be to develop within yourself a strong critical reflective attitude. Eventually the same standards of scrutiny and skepticism that you use regularly and intuitively in the daytime will become habitual in dreaming. In effect, you will sensitize yourself to the oddness of the dreamscape. The fact that you are dreaming will become more obvious, and lucid dreaming will become more and more common because it will take less and less to trigger lucidity. After all, from a lucid perspective, if you know that you went to bed recently and suddenly find yourself awake in some unexpected environment, the critical reflective mind will say, "Hey, I just went to bed! I'm not in the Los Angeles airport. This has to be a dream."

Complementary Strategies for Lucid Dreaming

WILD—Wake-Initiated Lucid Dreaming—provides a more direct approach to attaining lucidity, one that doesn't require all the daytime preparation of the MILD technique. If we surface from dreaming in the middle of the night, there is the possibility of either slipping back into our dream lucidly or of setting a strong intention to notice oddities or dream signs when we go back to sleep soon afterward. Below are three WILD practices.

As we saw in the previous chapter, sleep cycles last approximately ninety minutes and then repeat. Since the proportion of each cycle that contains dreams increases progressively throughout the night, if you find it easy to fall asleep, occasionally (when you don't have to go to work the next day) set your alarm so that you will awaken well into the night at a time when you are likely to be dreaming. Let's assume you are sleeping nine hours in a given night, which is equal to 540 minutes. Divided by ninety minutes per cycle, that comes to six cycles. If you set your alarm for four-and-a-half hours after you go to bed, you will awaken in 270 minutes—at the end of three sleep cycles. By this time your dream period in the latter part of each cycle has lengthened in comparison to earlier cycles. That means that when you awaken there is a good chance that you will be coming out of a dream of some length. Upon awakening set your alarm for ninety minutes later and go back to sleep with a strong resolve to become lucid. You can also try to lucidly reenter the dream you have just left, remembering and visualizing some of its details. If by now you have become skilled at remembering your dreams, this will come easily.

Continue in this manner, waking up in ninety-minute intervals and trying either to fall asleep into a dream lucidly or to prime yourself to recognize anomalies and dream signs. You come out of the dream awakened by the alarm, pause to reset your alarm, then use your momentary awakening to prime the lucid state upon reentering dreams. If your bedtime were 9 P.M., you would set your alarm for 1:30 A.M., then 3:00, then 4:30, then 6:00, then 7:30, and so on. Of course you can lengthen or shorten the total time. If you follow this practice you will soon discover for yourself that prime time for dreaming is in the later sleep sequences. It becomes much easier to enter dreams lucidly in those periods.

A second practice makes additional use of this fact. When you have time to sleep in, for instance on a weekend or holiday, take advantage of that by sleeping an additional ninety-minute sequence or two. If you are able to sleep that much, you will be having proportionately longer dreams in the later sequences, increasing your chances of becoming lucid. Once you have become proficient in lucid dreaming, these times will give you an opportunity to apply your skills and interests within long lucid dreams.

A third practice requires that you awaken well into the night and then remain awake for thirty to forty-five minutes before going back to sleep. Set your alarm to wake you after you have gone through several sleep cycles. Then get up and read something stimulating. The intention is to become very clearheaded. It would be most helpful if you were to read something associated with lucid dreaming so as to prime your interest in becoming lucid. This acts in the same way as prospective memory: you are creating an atmosphere of anticipation that will trigger lucidity later when you reenter sleep. Finally, set your intention to become lucid, and return to sleep. This has proven to be a very effective method for inducing lucid dreams.

Another WILD approach is to pay attention to hypnagogic imagery as you fall asleep. This can be done either when you fall asleep at bedtime or upon awakening during the night. If you are able to maintain some clarity—to stretch your attention a little further than normal into the process of falling asleep—you will be able to detect broken images, dreamlets, and a variety of visual patterns that are part of the process of losing consciousness as we fall asleep. These images occur in a space between initial drowsiness and light sleep (that is, during NREM 1). If we are able to maintain lucidity through this transition, we will find ourselves in NREM 2 and conscious of dreamless sleep.

Maintaining your attention on hypnagogic imagery requires that you observe in a very gentle and passive manner. View these images without becoming excited, making no attempt to hold onto or enhance them. If you can maintain this delicate balance, eventually full-fledged dreams may form from them. Remain passive, and simply allow yourself to be drawn into the dream. Preparing to fall asleep using the shamatha practice at the beginning of this chapter is very helpful in this approach. This type of WILD has much in common with the practices of dream yoga, which we will explore in later chapters.

Cultivating Lucidity Directly

One of the best ways to lay a firm foundation for attaining proficiency in lucid dreaming is to train in the shamatha technique of *settling the mind in its natural state*. In this practice one's attention is placed neither on the tactile sensations of the body nor on the breath but on the phenomena of the mind itself. That means that your object of attention will be the space of the mind and whatever thoughts, emotions, images, and other kinds of mental phenomena arise in that domain of experience. The goal is to simply observe this passing parade without becoming involved—without cultivating, investigating, being attracted to, encouraging, or rejecting any mental phenomena that appear in your mind. You maintain an even, calm presence whether those phenomena come fast and furious or few and far between. You have no preference as to what might appear. Just attend to whatever arises.

Using this practice as a complement to lucid dreaming makes perfect sense. Settling the mind in its natural state closely parallels the act of lucid dreaming. When you practice settling the mind in its natural state, you are becoming lucid to the mental activity of the waking state. You recognize these mental events as mental events, not mistaking them for events in the outer, intersubjective world. Normally we are as caught up in and carried away by our mental activities in the daytime as we are in the nocturnal mental activity we call dreaming. Rarely do we step back and simply observe our minds in action, becoming cognizant of the nature of the reality we are experiencing in the present moment. It makes sense, then, that if you can become lucid in your daytime experience, this will greatly facilitate lucidity when you're dreaming. Settling the mind in its natural state can also be effective for reentering dreams when you awaken at night.

Meditation Session for Settling the Mind in Its Natural State

Begin by settling the body in its natural state and the respiration in its natural rhythm as described in the first shamatha session in chapter 1:

Choose any comfortable **posture**—supine, seated cross-legged, or seated on a chair. If you are seated, be sure that your spine is straight and that your sternum is slightly uplifted so as to prevent any pressure on your abdomen that might keep the breath from moving freely. If you find any areas of muscular tension, breathe into them and then allow that tension to disperse on the exhalation. Finally, round off this initial settling of the body by taking three long, deep, refreshing breaths. Breathe down into the abdomen and expand upward through the diaphragm and chest. When your lungs are almost full, release your breath and let it flow out effortlessly.

Now scan your body from the crown of your head down to the tips of your toes with your attention not on any visual representation of your body but on the sensations experienced in each area. Then rest for a moment in the global experience of your body as a whole—as a **field of tactile sensations.** Next, concentrate on those areas of this field that are correlated with the breath—the rise and fall of the abdomen, diaphragm, chest, and any other movements associated with your breathing. Allow the breath to flow naturally, with your attention maintained throughout the entire inflow and outflow. Feel the release after the inhalation and the sensations as the air floods back into the body after the exhalation. Then **count twenty-one breaths,** concentrating not on the counting itself but on the sensations correlated with your breathing. This is a preliminary exercise for stabilizing and calming the mind.

Now open your eyes and let them remain at least partially open with your **gaze resting vacantly** in the space in front of you, and direct your attention to the space of the mind and whatever arises within that space. To facilitate this practice, at first you might generate a mental event or object, a thought or image, like that of a piece of fruit or the face of a relative— something familiar. Generate that image, focus single-pointedly upon that image, allow it to fade, then keep your attention right where it was, ready to detect the next image, thought, or mental event of any kind that arises within this space.

This practice is very simple: you do your best to **maintain an unwavering flow of mindfulness directed to the space of the**

mind, attending to whatever arises therein without reactivity, without judgment, without distraction or grasping.

You may experience intervals in which you are unable to detect any thought, image, or other mental event. Yet you still have an object of meditation: during those intervals between thoughts simply attend to—with discerning mindfulness—the vacuity of the space of the mind. You are attending both to the stage and to the players on the stage. So when there are no players, attend to the stage.

When you notice that you have become distracted—falling into the habits of becoming involved with thoughts, encouraging new thoughts, emotions, or images, reacting to mental phenomena—step back gently into the mindful and passive observation of the mental flow.

After twenty-four minutes, bring the practice to a close.

OUTLINE OF THE PRACTICE:

- Posture: your choice (supine, seated cross-legged, seated on a chair)
- Body: settled in its natural state
- Breathing: settled in its natural state
- Attention: on the space of the mind and whatever mental events that arise in that domain of experience[2]
- When distracted: relax, release whatever captivated your attention, then return your awareness to the space of the mind and its contents
- Length: one ghatika (twenty-four minutes)
- Intention: to attend to mental phenomena with lucidity as a preparation for lucid dreaming; to develop concentration using mental phenomena as the object of attention

Putting It All Together

The three essential requirements for learning to dream lucidly are (1) adequate motivation, (2) correct practice of effective techniques, and (3) excellent dream recall. The goal is to become proficient in lucid dreaming. That means having frequent lucid dreams and extending their length so that you have the time to pursue the activities that brought you to lucid dreaming in the first place. Using once more the metaphor of the laboratory—yours won't be of much use to you if the lab is open only once or twice a month and then only for a few minutes at a time. Many students of lucid dreaming who make the effort not only are able to extend their lucid dreams to half an hour and more but can have them pretty much at will. So after you have opened the door to lucid dreaming—once you've tasted the experience—the next phase is to stabilize that environment and start using it.

4

Proficiency in Lucid Dreaming

EXTENDING YOUR LUCID DREAMS

By now you may have had a few lucid dreams. In the beginning your biggest problem may have been getting used to the thrill of suddenly finding yourself awake in a dream, so that your excitement didn't immediately awaken you. You have probably floated or flown around in your dreams, defying the law of gravity. Perhaps you have noticed how numbers and letters in the dream world usually change when you look at them a second time. These are, of course, two of the main state checks you can use to determine if you are dreaming or not. Likely, at some point not far into your dream, the scenario has either suddenly or gradually broken up or faded and you've awakened. Or your attention has faded and you have either lost lucidity—being swept into ordinary dreaming—or you have blacked out into dreamless sleep. These are the two main obstacles to extending lucid dreams: losing your lucid awareness of the dream and losing the dream itself.

KEEPING THE DREAM ALIVE

Lucid dream research suggests that the fading or break-up of dreams into either the waking experience or into dreamless sleep is a matter of one sensory stimulus gaining the upper hand on another. Losing the dream means that either waking sensory input or the extremely low-key (essentially unconscious) input from dreamless sleep for one reason or another becomes dominant. Sensory information from non-dream environments gradually infiltrates or simply floods your mental perception. The antidote to this intrusion on your lucid dreams is to refocus your attention on the sensations of the dream. Several methods have proved extremely effective for reconstituting dreams as they begin to destabilize.

If, as you dream lucidly, you sense that the visual scenario of the dream is losing its integrity, **spin your dream body** with your eyes wide open. This brisk, gyrating motion will cause your senses to be flooded by the images and sensations of the dream environment. In a very high percentage of cases, either this maneuver will cause the dream you were in previously to reconstitute or you will have spun yourself into a new dream scenario. As such, spinning can also be used as a means to change dreams—to skip from dream to dream.

Another time-tested method is to **give your dream body a rubdown.** In most cases when you dream lucidly, "you" are located in a close replica of your ordinary body. The feel of this dream body is similar to your waking body. Since you have dream hands, simply rub the skin of your dream body vigorously. As with spinning, the flood of sensory information will override the waking or dreamless sleep stimulus that is interrupting your lucid dream.

Following the same logic of boosting the relative volume of dream phenomena, you can also **concentrate your focus on some object within the dream.** Many of your dream objects may be shifting relatively rapidly—people, cars, even the background scenery itself. But your dream body and the ground upon which you are standing will tend to be more stable. Focusing so that they become more vivid will anchor you within the dream, causing any competing data from the waking state or dreamless sleep to fade out. So the key to stabilizing a dream that starts to become shaky is to heighten your engagement with the dream itself.

KEEPING LUCIDITY ALIVE

Loss of lucidity means, in essence, that you have lost touch with the reality of your situation. Instead of maintaining awareness that you are dreaming—that your body is lying motionless in bed while you are awake to your dreams—you once again believe the dream is real. It is amazing how easily this can happen. Even in the most bizarre dream circumstances, the sluggishness of untrained dream consciousness uncritically accepts everything. If you were in Denver one moment and Los Angeles the next, and you begin to question that, the voice of dream dullness will justify it—successfully—with thoughts like, "Oh yeah. I must have taken a plane," or "I must be mistaken about having been in Denver," and so forth. So maintaining the critical reflective attitude that is the main support for lucidity in dreaming requires a great deal of vigilance, because you are going against one of the strongest habits of human life—snug, comfy "sleepy time." We love to curl up our bodies and shut down our minds at bedtime—just like cats and dogs do—and we've been doing it all our lives.

Of course, the more you **train in shamatha,** the less likely you are to lose lucidity in dreams. The simple practice of following your breath requires that you avoid the ingrained tendency to follow thoughts obliviously. Beyond basic shamatha, settling the mind in its natural state, as shown previously, is precisely the maintenance of a critically reflective attitude. If you are accustomed to this in daytime—and especially if you can gain some mastery, making it a habit—you will have less trouble maintaining lucidity at night.

The most basic way to ensure that you maintain lucidity in dreams is to **repeat to yourself frequently, "This is a dream,"**

or "I am dreaming." Just keep reminding yourself. This will prevent you from getting caught up in some dream detail, which can easily lure you away from lucidity. While lucid, it may happen that you will latch onto something odd or seductive that piques your interest. Maybe it's a vintage sports car you wanted to own, an attractive member of the opposite sex, your favorite dessert, an incredible sunset over the sea. Next thing you know you are wining and dining the lover of your dreams—and you have become so interested that *it is real.* Lucidity? Out the door! It is possible in such situations to have your cake and eat it too— "My darling, isn't this a dream?"—but only if your critical faculty matches the strength of your interest and desires.

The same thing can happen in nightmares—where you may have a strong desire to put an end to the dream. If you find yourself dreaming lucidly in what you consider horrid circumstances, and you choose not to confront it, the easiest way out of the dream is to close your (dream) eyes. This, incidentally, is a technique for entering lucid dreamless sleep. If you have the skill you can escape by flying to another self-created planet or galaxy, or transform the nightmarish situation or apparition into something less frightening. You could turn a werewolf into a snuggly kitten or a fiery volcano into a fountain.

PSYCHOLOGICAL INSIGHTS

However, you may also take the approach of changing your *reaction* to such a dream. You can remind yourself that you are dreaming and that any apparently threatening object in your dream is nonexistent. Using patience and relaxation in such situations, you may be able to strengthen yourself psychologically—and perhaps gain some wisdom. We'll explore these possibilities more deeply in the section on dream yoga.

You may have noticed that by anticipating something within a lucid dream, that event will take place. In my case, when I find myself in one of my "anxious traveler" dreams, become lucid, and catch myself thinking, "I think I've missed my flight," I'll glance out the airport window and, sure enough, there goes my plane taking off from the runway. I may know that I am dreaming and that the airport is not real, but there goes my plane anyway. You can **use anticipation consciously to maintain lucidity.** If, for instance, you think, "I bet my best friend Carl is going to walk through the door now," often that is precisely what will happen. Then you can link such self-fulfilling prophesies into sequences. "Now Carl is going to play an accordion. The accordion is going to turn into a vintage Ferrari, and we are going to drive the coast of the French Riviera. Perhaps there will be a sunset. . . . Oh look! There it is!," and so on.

This is one method of creating stories and continuity within your lucid dreams. Another way is to set up a specific intention, as in "Tonight, I am going to climb Mt. Everest." In daytime, practice anticipating that you will be dreaming the mountain climb. Look at pictures of Mt. Everest, read about those who have climbed it, flip through catalogs of mountain climbing equipment, and so forth. Think of a plan for climbing the mountain—setting up your base camp, choosing a particular route, solutions to specific difficulties along the way, and so on. Set your intention strongly at bedtime, repeating over and over without any other distractions that you will find yourself at the base of Mt. Everest when you dream, and that you will then climb it following your plan. Once again you are using prospective memory—this time in an elaborate form—to reach and maintain lucidity.

Lucid Dreamless Sleep

Dreamless sleep, as we saw in chapter 2, is normally a state that we enter naturally and unconsciously and in which we remain with a very low level of awareness, if any at all. (These natural dreamless states are denoted NREM 2, 3, and 4 in the generalized sleep pattern mentioned earlier.) It is, however, a state we can explore and benefit from, if we take a keen interest in understanding the nature of consciousness and mental states. Lucid dreamless sleep brings us a relatively pure experience of the substrate. Although the substrate is termed vacuous, it is not completely empty, not completely unconfigured. Since in the sleep cycle dreams naturally develop out of dreamless sleep, entering this arena consciously, or becoming lucid after having entered there, gives us the opportunity to observe the embryonic development of a dream.

In more advanced practices, the development of stability in lucid dreamless sleep can be a crucial factor in one's navigating the after-death bardo.[1] In Tibetan Buddhism it is believed that this after-death state is a factor determining the nature of one's rebirth. Normally the consciousness of the deceased is confused and frightened by the unfamiliar and dramatic appearances of this bardo—unable to either comprehend it or use it to effect a more positive rebirth. However, if one has attained stability in dreamless sleep, there is a better chance that one can remain calm in this situation and make meaningful choices—especially if one has prepared oneself by studying texts explaining the nature of this transitional state.

One exercise you can perform in the state of lucid dreamless sleep is to address your attention to the vacuity (the substrate) and pose questions such as, "What is the nature of this vacuity? What is its size, shape? What are its characteristics?" Having observed the substrate, resting there, answers to these questions can bring you to a bigger one: "What is the nature of being conscious?" In this rarified atmosphere, devoid of distractions, you can examine consciousness in detail and perhaps find important answers to questions that have puzzled philosophers for millennia.

Another advanced practice based on lucid dreamless sleep is *open presence,* which falls under the heading of Dzogchen, a topic we will examine in a later chapter. In brief, if one is able to attain stability in lucid dreamless sleep, accessing the substrate, practicing open presence may enable one to break through to pristine awareness—one's buddha-nature. For those on the spiritual path, this is a major accomplishment.

The Practice of Awareness of Awareness (or Shamatha without a Sign)

One way to directly enter lucid dreamless sleep is to close one's eyes during the activities of normal lucid dreaming. This brings one immediately to the vacuity of the substrate. Another method, found in dream yoga, is to concentrate on a visualized image at the heart chakra. Below I will give a method from the practice of shamatha called awareness of awareness, which allows the meditator to gently sink into dreamless sleep lucidly at bedtime.

A Session of Awareness of Awareness: Begin as in previous shamatha sessions by settling the body in its natural state. Find a **comfortable posture**—either sitting or lying in the supine position. Then, after taking three deep, luxurious breaths, **settle your breathing in its natural rhythm.** As you practice mindfulness of breathing, let your eyes be at least partially open and rest your gaze in the space before you, paying no attention to objects near or far. Continue breathing comfortably and gently attune yourself to the qualities of relaxation, stillness, and vigilance. Be peripherally aware of any mental phenomena that pass through your mind's eye.

Once you have attained a state that is relaxed and even, release your attention to all objects—any and all mental and physical appearances—and settle your awareness in the very state of being aware. Your awareness is not directed anywhere, neither inward nor outward, but rests naturally in its own nature. Whatever thoughts arise, release them immediately. You are allowing your awareness to settle naturally into its own nature. As you maintain this relaxed, easy vigilance, simply release any phenomena that obscure the clarity of your awareness.

What's left over is the sheer event of knowing. From time to time, check to see that you are not straining and that your breathing remains deeply relaxed. Rest in this state of utter simplicity.

After one ghatika, bring the session to a close. (If you are using this meditation as a dream practice at bedtime, start in the supine position. Then, once you have achieved stability, roll over and allow yourself to fall asleep while maintaining your attention on awareness alone.)

OUTLINE OF THE PRACTICE:

- Settle your body in its natural state
- Settle your breathing in its natural rhythm
- Rest evenly—relaxed, still, and vigilant
- Release any thoughts that come to mind
- Settle awareness on awareness alone
- Length: one ghatika (or the time it takes to fall asleep lucidly)
- Intention: to explore the limpid clarity of the substrate consciousness, possibly as a prelude to a breakthrough to pristine awareness; or to enter into lucid dreamless sleep

COMMENTARY

This practice is utterly simple. The attention must be maintained in a very quiet and subtle manner, especially if your intention is to fall asleep lucidly. Once you have gained some mastery of this practice, the substrate consciousness is experienced directly, imbued with the qualities of bliss, luminosity, and nonconceptuality. Awareness of awareness provides a shortcut to this experience, which is achieved more gradually over time through the practice of settling the mind in its natural state.

Given that this practice is so subtle, how can you be sure you are maintaining awareness of awareness? It is helpful for any kind of practice to know what the extremes are so you can cleave a middle path between them. For this one, if you try too hard this gives rise to agitation and if you don't try hard enough you fall into dullness. Once you recognize the two extremes, you want to do something in between, which means bouncing off of those extremes more and more lightly. If you are focusing on any object, a thought or an image, this is one extreme, on the agitation side. The other extreme, which is more elusive, is sitting there with a blank mind not aware of anything. You are not attending to any object—just vegetating. What is in between is a quality of freshness because you are located in the present moment and vividly aware. You are not attending to any object at all but are aware that awareness is happening. It is wonderfully simple but subtle. It is like slipping into an old pair of shoes. When you are in it, you really know you are there. You need to develop a confidence that you know when you are doing it correctly. This is how it is done.

The Dream Lab

Once you have developed enough experience, and the frequency, stability, and vividness of your dreams reach a certain threshold, you may create dream laboratories in which to carry out activities of interest to you. If, for instance, you are keen on science, you could run thought experiments in a highly imaginative way. Many of the great scientific insights took place not during an experiment but while the scientist was being free with the imagination. Newton's apple—which reportedly gave him the idea that gravity was a force of attraction—is a prime example. Albert Einstein used imagination (of course a very well-informed imagination) to predict the outcome of experiments, some of which were performed many years after his formulations. His vision of gravity as curved space—which turned Newton's view on its head—seems to have been generated as an imaginative reframing of the question, "What is gravity?" In lucid dreams one can manipulate environments and the objects within them in a very fluid and vivid manner, ideally suited for anything from the design of experiments to the kind of free-form imagining important to cutting-edge science.

This same example would apply to engineers and inventors, who could conceivably devise and try out their designs in the three-dimensional "holodeck" of controlled lucid dreaming. We'll look at some practical implications of lucid dreaming in greater detail in a later chapter.

A Space for Meditation

There are a great variety of meditation techniques, many of which require a quiet space where one can meditate for relatively long periods of time without distractions. Traditionally, caves and cabins in remote locations have been the preferred settings. Still, even those places can present difficulties when it comes to procuring food, extreme conditions such as cold and dampness, and the dangers if one were to become seriously ill in such a remote location. Handling these problems is a test for determined meditators, perhaps an integral part of their growth toward maturity in the arduous path to spiritual realization.

However, what could be more ideal than to develop a space within your lucid dreams where you could meditate without distractions? If you desired a visual space conducive to your practice, you could provide yourself a room, a cave, a mountain-top with a glorious view—whatever your desires and skill level in lucid dreaming allowed. If you wished, the walls could be adorned with images relating to your style of practice—a life-like statue of the Buddha, Shiva, Jesus, or whomever. You could go so far as to place a rug and a pillow to sit upon—although you could just as easily hover in the air. If your practice involved visualization, with practice you could reproduce in three dimensions the most elaborate images.

Again, the key here is stability and vividness: Most will have to increase their lucid dream time gradually to enable them to practice up to an hour in this mind-made environment without losing either the dream or its lucid quality. Vividness—the sharpness of images and their color and clarity—also takes time to develop, unless one is naturally gifted in the way many visual artists are. If you wish to meditate in the space of lucid dreaming you will begin by focusing your determination by affirming—in the same manner you learned lucid dreaming in the first place—"Tonight I will create a quiet space for meditation in my dreams."

Of course, you don't have to create anything as elaborate as a meditation cave in order to meditate while practicing lucid dreaming. If you wish to do the shamatha practice of following your breath, just imagine a dream body that breathes and follow that breathing. If you possessed the stability to create a visual image, such as a candle flame, a jewel, or even an image that is sacred to you, you could develop concentration and eventually arrive at samadhi (meditative concentration) by maintaining your attention exclusively on that image for progressively longer periods.

Another ideal meditation practice for lucid dreaming is settling the mind in its natural state. In this case, as we saw earlier, you do not alter or control any of the mental phenomena that appear to you. Since everything perceived in the dream state—thoughts, emotions, and physical objects—are mental, you simply pay attention to everything that arises without grasping, without being carried away. This will naturally strengthen your stability as a lucid dreamer since, as we saw previously, being lucid to the appearance of all phenomena—day and night—is the fundamental template for lucid dreaming. So doing this practice while dreaming has the double advantage of increasing your skill in an important, fundamental meditation technique with wide applications to spiritual practice, and also strengthening your ability to dream lucidly.

PART TWO

Dream Yoga

5

The Universe of Dream Yoga

A S WE HAVE SEEN, lucid dreaming is a relative newcomer in the field of modern psychology. Initially developed by specialists in sleep research—a subfield of psychology—over the past three decades it has gained enthusiastic adherents among the lay public, though most academic psychologists have expressed surprisingly little interest in this provocative line of research. That may be because it is seen as too subjective and therefore unworthy of scientific inquiry.[1] Given the malleability of lucid dreams and the variety of human interests, the range of activities one may engage in while dreaming is infinite. Lucid dreamers may view their nocturnal adventures as anything from an exotic hobby to a spiritual quest.

In contrast, the field of dream yoga is a specific spiritual practice embedded in a worldview dating back two and a half millennia—the Buddhist worldview. That universe, which is complex while at the same time well integrated, is driven by the twin goals of relieving the suffering of all beings and of hastening their enlightenment. The literature of this altruistic Buddhist psychology is immense, and within it there are numerous texts on dream yoga, not to mention oral teaching passed down over centuries. Although one need not become a Buddhist to practice dream yoga, some knowledge of Buddhism's aims and methods is essential. Keep in mind also that there is an overlap between lucid dreaming and dream yoga. Even if your dreaming goals do not involve spiritual practice, you will find some of the practices of dream yoga useful as a means of sharpening your abilities as a lucid dreamer. Indeed, some of the specific techniques are nearly identical. In like manner, those interested in dream practice from a spiritual perspective can benefit from the more easily assimilated instructions of lucid dreaming. In that sense the two practices are complementary.

"Awake" Means What?

The most dramatic difference between lucid dreaming and dream yoga hinges on what it means to be lucid or awake. The Western scientific tradition from which psychological theories and practices of lucid dreaming developed considers the normal waking state to be as awake as one can get: at night we go to sleep and enter into an "unreal" dreamworld. In the morning when we awaken we once again perceive reality more or less "as it is." That's all there is to it. We may become lucid while dreaming, but that awakening is not viewed as substantially different from the mental clarity of daytime. One is simply awake to the dreaming process.

Buddhism, however, considers normal waking consciousness itself to be a dream state relative to our deepest dimension of consciousness. The Buddhist hypothesis here is that among three general states of consciousness—waking, sleeping, and dreaming—the coarsest state of consciousness, the one with the least potential for spiritual development, with the least malleability, is, surprisingly, the ordinary waking state. In terms of the quest for spiritual advancement, what we are normally experiencing is the worst. The dream state has more potential, but if we fail to recognize the dream state for what it is, we inevitably mistake it for the waking state and proceed through the dream in a state of delusion. Dreamless sleep entails an even subtler dimension of awareness that could be used to great advantage on the spiritual path, but it is usually so obscured by lack of clarity that we can't tap into the full potential of this consciousness. Above and beyond those three states, as we normally experience them, are numerous states of progressively more awakened consciousness that we can develop. But one is not considered to be truly "awake" until one achieves enlightenment—the state of a buddha, in which one has awakened to the deepest dimension of consciousness. For Buddhism, *that* is as awake as one can get. Until we attain the full awakening of buddhahood, we are asleep.

AN EMPIRICAL TRADITION

Whatever our personal definition of "awake" may be, if we wish to borrow ideas from Buddhism's dream yoga to help us awaken within our dreams, we are in luck, because several key Buddhist concepts nicely parallel modern thinking. To begin with, Buddhism is an empirical tradition—Buddhists are warned against uncritically accepting the teachings on faith alone. Rather, they are encouraged to test the hypotheses. The Buddha himself said to his monks: "Just as the wise accept gold after testing it by heating, cutting, and rubbing it, so are my words to be accepted after examining them, but not out of respect for me."[2] That statement should ring a bell for all of us brought up in the Western tradition, which is ideally based on logical reasoning, experience (i.e., experimentation), and objective, factual data. The demand for solid proof is central to our heritage, so much so that one American state (Missouri) calls itself the "Show-Me State." It wouldn't be far-fetched to call Buddhism the "show-me religion." The practices of Buddhism, including dream yoga, are there to be proven by personal experience.

Psychology: The Psyche and Beyond

Another area of interest shared by Buddhism and modern Western society is psychology. Western psychology seeks to understand the *psyche*. The psychologist Carl Jung defined the psyche as "the totality of all psychic processes, conscious as well as unconscious." For Freud it comprised the largely unconscious *id* and the moralizing conscious of the *super-ego,* both mediated and integrated by the *ego*. According to the *American Heritage Medical Dictionary,*[3] the psyche is "the mind functioning as the center of thought, emotion, and behavior and consciously or unconsciously mediating the body's responses to the social and physical environment."

If mapping and understanding the psyche so defined are the primary goals of Western psychology, in Buddhist psychology, as suggested earlier, the psyche is but one province on a more extensive map, a broader understanding of the mind. And we've seen that Buddhist psychology got a two-thousand-year jump on the West, which has taken the study of the mind seriously for only about a century and a half. So Buddhism has an abundance of fascinating research to offer us—hypotheses and practices that we may apply both to our dreams and to waking reality.

As one might expect, this difference in scope parallels the difference between lucid dreaming and dream yoga and is a key to integrating the two disciplines in practice. Since lucid dreaming follows the tenets of Western psychology, it considers the psyche as its field of activity. From that viewpoint, when you dream lucidly you are experiencing and exploring the psyche. The phenomena you encounter there and the way that field operates can be viewed through the lens of Western psychology and its theories and concepts.

The Substrate Consciousness

Dream yoga seeks to go beyond the psyche, eventually to *primordial consciousness,*[4] which, when fully realized, is synonymous with the ultimate goal of Buddhism itself—enlightenment. Before one arrives there, however, we encounter a state of consciousness more subtle than the psyche, though not as transcendent as primordial consciousness. This second mental field, the *substrate consciousness* (Sanskrit: *alaya vijñana*),[5] is different from the subconscious of Freud and the collective consciousness of Jung. It is prior to and more fundamental than the subconscious—a sub-subconscious. As such, it is considered to be the source of the entire psyche, including what we Westerners call the subconscious. Therefore there is some overlap between the psyche and the substrate consciousness, although the latter concept presents a deeper and more detailed picture of what Western psychologists call the unconscious. This is why lucid dreamers may benefit from the theory and practice of dream yoga.

Although the substrate consciousness is unique to the individual—distinguishing it from Jung's collective unconscious[6]—for Buddhism it is the basis for subsequent incarnations. It could be said that it is not the individual that reincarnates but successive expressions of an individual continuum of a substrate consciousness. This mental stream begins to become configured at conception and is then modified by the thinking, emotions, behavior, and experiences of the individual being throughout one's life. Roughly speaking, these behaviors are stored in the substrate consciousness as karmic imprints that condition the life of the individual as well as future incarnations. Wholesome behavior imprints positive karma leading to a more positive future and possible evolution toward enlightenment. Nonvirtuous activities imprint negative karma—seeds that result in negative outcomes in the future. Therefore, the substrate consciousness is similar to a computer memory chip, where previous inputs constantly modify the present and condition the future operation of the computer. Just as the software and hardware of a computer constantly interact with and influence each other, so do the substrate consciousness and its emergent psyche causally interact with each other throughout the course of a lifetime.

The relevance of the substrate consciousness for dream yoga is its power over our understanding. As the source of all ordinary mental phenomena, ignorance of its operation prevents us from seeing how we stand in our own way, blocking our own progress, in our quest for wisdom, virtue, and happiness. Penetration of the substrate consciousness reveals the inner terrain that must be transformed in the process of spiritual maturation. Our fears, misconceptions, memories, latent tendencies, and so forth are all stored in the substrate consciousness. When phobias and neuroses, delusions and misinterpretations arise, they emanate from this same source. Furthermore, the *qualia* that we perceive by way of our senses actually emerge from the substrate, the empty, luminous space of experience that is directly perceived by the substrate consciousness. This space is vividly cognized when one experiences deep, dreamless sleep lucidly, that is, recognizing this state for what it is while one is fast asleep. Explored wisely, the substrate and substrate consciousness become the gateway to wisdom and to enlightenment. Dream yoga provides direct access to this realm and a means of transforming it.

PRIMORDIAL CONSCIOUSNESS

A thorough exploration of the substrate consciousness, together with the psyche it subsumes, provides a "launching pad" for probing the deepest space of awareness, primordial consciousness. Primordial consciousness transcends all concepts, including those of subject and object, existence and nonexistence. It is timeless and "unborn" into the relative universe we conceive of as "existence." It is the source of virtues such as compassion, creativity, and wisdom, which emanate from it spontaneously. The full realization of primordial consciousness is the achievement of total freedom, enlightenment—the final victory. This is the ultimate aim of dream yoga and of all genuine Buddhist practice.

The substrate consciousness is highly conditioned, a repository of innate tendencies, karmic propensities—the basis of samsara. In contrast, primordial consciousness represents total freedom from such mental afflictions. Primordial consciousness, or ultimate *bodhichitta*, is nondual from relative bodhichitta—the wish to achieve buddhahood in order to bring all other sentient beings[7] to enlightenment. In the traditional Mahayana[8] practice of relative bodhichitta, one gradually develops great love and compassion for all sentient beings. This can be achieved through exercises that lead one to first see other sentient beings as equal in value to ourselves (a big step beyond our normally self-centered viewpoint), and finally to view other sentient beings collectively as of greater value than ourselves. Our orientation becomes one of helping others to the greatest extent possible based on the recognition of their suffering and of their potential for happiness. This training is largely conceptual. However, through the realization of primordial consciousness, great compassion and relative bodhichitta—the aspiration to achieve perfect enlightenment for the sake of all beings— arise spontaneously. You don't need to look elsewhere, outside of ultimate bodhichitta, to find relative bodhichitta.

SUPPORTS IN THE QUEST FOR ENLIGHTENMENT

It is of supreme importance to an understanding of Buddhism to know that the Buddha's first teaching after his enlightenment was on the subject of suffering. This teaching, given in the Deer Park at Sarnath near Varanasi, India, is called the Four Noble Truths. Stated simply, these are (1) the reality of suffering, (2) the reality of suffering fundamentally resulting from the inner cause of ignorance, (3) the reality that suffering and its causes can be eradicated, and (4) the path that leads to the end of suffering. Until the third noble truth is realized, we are bound to suffering by ignorance, which is its fundamental cause.

Since its ultimate aim is none other than enlightenment as

defined by the Buddhist tradition, dream yoga is supported by the same philosophy and practices that are essential to the overall Tibetan Buddhist path. Tibetan Buddhism incorporates all three of the main Buddhist traditions: (1) the *Shravakayana*, with its emphasis on the realization of one's own individual liberation; (2) the *Mahayana*, where the perfect enlightenment of a buddha is sought for the sake of all beings; and (3) the *Vajrayana* (including the Great Perfection, Dzogchen), which unites emptiness with expression, that is, although all phenomena are empty of inherent existence, they are at the same time pure manifestations of enlightened mind. Traditionally, students of Tibetan Buddhism have been taught the older traditions such as the Shravakayana and related schools, then been introduced to the Mahayana, and finally to the more advanced practices of Vajrayana. Whether or not one has passed through these sequentially, any in-depth study of Tibetan Buddhism will bring one into contact with all three approaches, unified into a consistent whole.

Emptiness—which is not to be confused with the nihilistic idea of nothingness—can be defined as the lack both of inherent existence of phenomena and of an intrinsic duality between subject and object. The personal self, for example, is not an absolute that exists monolithically, to be found in some distinct and unchanging form or location. What we choose to call our "self" changes from moment to moment and is dependent on any number of factors such as one's mood, one's immediate situation, one's family, one's culture and nationality, and so on. Deep and careful investigation reveals no single, all-encompassing "I." The "I" as an inherently existing entity, independent of conceptual designation, is *empty*. That, in a nutshell, is the emptiness of the personal self.

The same can be said of phenomena that are not normally labeled as part of the personal self. For example, we tend to reify the existence of all kinds of objects even though they have no stable or independent identity in time. A simple object such as a teacup was not so long ago some clay, and before that, solid minerals and water. In the future the teacup will be broken pieces of pottery, barely identifiable fragments, then dust. Even if a teacup were preserved intact for millennia, a future civilization that didn't drink tea might have no idea what it was or identify it as something else. If it were thought to be a spittoon, for instance, that is what it would become. Objects are no more than labels, their validity deriving from general consensus within a given community. They are empty of any absolute or inherent identity. When we search for the objects themselves as something inherent and immutable, they are not found.

Furthermore, the emptiness of all phenomena is not viewed as some absolute, underlying basis for phenomena. Search for emptiness and it too is nowhere to be found, itself empty of inherent existence. Emptiness is merely the ultimate manner in which phenomena exist. Moreover, the existence of experienced phenomena is dependent upon the sensory organs that detect them and minds that conceive of them. So in an important sense, all phenomena are co-emergent with the modes of awareness that apprehend them. To the mind of a bird, the object that we call a "mosquito" is a type of food. To humans a mosquito can be anything from a wonder to an irritant to a danger (especially if it carries a dangerous disease). To a mosquito, we humans are food—a source of blood needed to fertilize the female mosquito's eggs. But what is the absolute meaning of "mosquito"? The mosquito is empty of any ultimate or absolute meaning. Emptiness is nothing more than the lack of inherent existence that becomes evident when phenomena are placed under careful analysis. Emptiness is an essential feature of mentally conditioned existence. It is our ignorance of this feature that leads us astray and is a main source of suffering. By believing in the intrinsic existence of phenomena we, in a sense, take things too seriously. We will become more deeply acquainted with emptiness in the following chapters.

Since treading the Buddhist path to enlightenment requires

an ethical foundation, ethics is relevant to the practice of dream yoga. The foundation of ethics in Tibetan Buddhism is the intention to avoid injuring anyone and to be of service when the opportunity arises. Beyond that, ethical conduct prevents the accumulation of negative karma, which would impede the individual's quest for enlightenment (and bring adverse circumstances to one's life in general). Ethical conduct is also one of the guarantors of the kind of tranquil mind required for advanced Buddhist practice. If one is nagged by guilt and guile in one's daily life, such tranquility is unlikely. Persons dominated by competitiveness, pride, anger, jealousy, and so forth will find it difficult to access subtle states of consciousness requiring a stable, tranquil mind.

Buddhism has numerous guidelines for ethical conduct. One is the Ten Non-virtues, a list of behaviors to be avoided. They are the non-virtues of the body: (1) killing, (2) stealing, (3) sexual misconduct (generally meaning sexual conduct that brings suffering to others); the non-virtues of speech: (4) lying, (5) harsh speech, (6) slander, (7) idle chatter; and the non-virtues of mind: (8) wishing harm, (9) coveting, and (10) wrong views (i.e., views not in harmony with reality). The Six Perfections comprise a list of virtuous activities directly related to advancement on the spiritual path. One is encouraged to practice (1) generosity, (2) ethical discipline, (3) patience, (4) enthusiasm, (5) meditation, and (6) wisdom. The Four Immeasurable Virtues comprise a list of positive aspirations for the well-being of all sentient beings. One cultivates the aspirations with the greatest sincerity possible: (1) "May all sentient beings have happiness and its causes," (2) "May all sentient beings be free from suffering and its causes," (3) "May all sentient beings never be separated from the happiness that is without suffering," and (4) "May all sentient beings abide in equanimity, free of attachment and aversion."

These and other formulations reveal that altruism is the basis of the Tibetan Buddhist path to enlightenment. They are expressions of bodhichitta, the desire to achieve enlightenment so that all sentient beings may be relieved of all suffering and be brought to ultimate happiness, epitomized by the wish, "May I achieve enlightenment for the benefit of all sentient beings, that I may bring them all to enlightenment." Practices of bodhichitta include those where one gives other beings equal value to oneself and those where one places others entirely above oneself. For example, one guide, the *Eight Verses of Thought Transformation*,[9] states: "When in the company of others, I shall always consider myself the lowest of all, and from the depths of my heart hold others dear and supreme." Although this may seem from the outside to be a radical self-denial or even self-denigration, as the Dalai Lama has often stated, such a stance of cherishing others more than oneself can remove the burden of self-centeredness. If the weight of egotism can occasionally strain even a confirmed egotist—and there is plenty of evidence to that effect—it can certainly hamper those on spiritual paths requiring the tranquility derived from purity of heart.

PRAGMATISM

The path to enlightenment, the eradication of suffering, ethical conduct, bodhichitta, and so forth are lofty ideals. But Buddhism aims above all else to put these into practice. The Buddha practiced to achieve his enlightenment, and his ideas were always backed up by specific advice through which his students achieved some degree of realization. Faith is not enough. The practices must bear the intended fruit. Through dream yoga, the yogi can directly recognize the emptiness of the personal self and of phenomena. Dream yoga can prepare one for the after-death bardo, touched on earlier. The phenomena of this bardo can be either obstacles or aids to spiritual advancement depending on the strength and direction of one's practices in life. If one has a thorough understanding of the dream state and can control one's dreams, this can be done in the after-death bardo as well.

Dream yoga, when supported by the achievement of shamatha, can also give one access to supernatural powers such as clairaudience, clairvoyance, and precognition. These are important for those who teach the Buddhist Dharma. A teacher with direct access to the thoughts of his students will be far more precise in providing counsel appropriate to each. The direct contact with the substrate consciousness afforded by the achievement of shamatha and dream yoga allows one to access memories from previous lifetimes. It is also theoretically possible that the dream yogi may receive teachings from realized beings in dreams. There have been many examples of this recorded in the history of diverse contemplative traditions, including Buddhism. On the face of it, to a citizen of the modern world this may seem absurd. But when one examines the kinds of material revealed in these cases, along with the apparent sanity, indeed genius of the recipients of such teachings—not to mention their evident integrity and lack of motive for fabrication—one's skepticism may diminish.

Tibetan Buddhism—Vajrayana especially—incorporates a physiological approach to spiritual attainment. The basis here is the "channels, vital energies, and vital essences." These structures, which may have correlates in the Chinese arts involving *chi* (acupuncture, Chi Gong, and Tai Chi, for example), along with other ancient medical and spiritual traditions, have not (as yet) been identified by science. Nonetheless, their positive effects on health are evident, even to Western medicine. Access to the channels, vital energies, and vital essences—as well as to chakras, or energy centers—often comes through visualization. Dream yoga employs these elements and their attendant visualizations to evoke these physiological aides for the explorations of dreams and dreamless sleep. We will examine these topics next, as we learn the practices of Tibetan dream yoga.

6

The Daytime Practices
of Dream Yoga

THE DREAM YOGA TEACHINGS
OF PADMASAMBHAVA

Just as one prepares during the day for nighttime lucid dreaming—doing state checks, keeping a dream journal, developing a critical reflective attitude, and so forth—the dream yogi uses daytime dream yoga practices to prepare the ground for nighttime dream yoga. For both styles of practice, if you can become lucid during the waking state and make that a habit, you will much more easily attain lucidity while dreaming. However, as we have seen, the awakening sought in dream yoga—both day and night—embraces a much wider range of experience than does lucid dreaming.

One lineage of classic teachings on dream yoga was brought to Tibet by the eighth-century Indian adept Padmasambhava. A master of all of the practices of the Buddhist "diamond vehicle," or Vajrayana, many of his teachings were passed down to future generations as *terma* (Tibetan for "treasure"), placed in the ground, in solid rock, in lakes, and even in the minds of those who later discovered these treasures, who are called *tertöns*. Padmasambhava's teachings on dream yoga given here come from just such a terma—a cycle of teachings entitled *Natural Liberation,* secreted like a time capsule into a boulder and unearthed by the tertön Karma Lingpa, some six hundred years after Padmasambhava's time in Tibet. Both the day and night dream yoga teachings found in *Natural Liberation* presume a degree of mental vividness and stability derived from developed powers of concentration. Therefore, it was Padmasambhava's opinion that a subtle and serviceable mind, one honed by practicing shamatha, is indispensable for success in the practice of dream yoga.

GETTING REAL

Padmasambhava's teachings on dream yoga begin with the provocative statement, "It is like this: all phenomena are nonexistent, but they appear to exist and are established as various things." At first glance that may seem a bit shocking—even crazy. But taken in context it makes sense. By "nonexistent," Padmasambhava is not speaking nihilistically—he is not telling us that nothing exists whatsoever. Rather, he is inviting us to change our perspective on not only dream phenomena but waking experience as well. He is suggesting that our normal waking experience is just as deluded and fantastic as our dreams. This is precisely the view of emptiness we touched on earlier, for the phenomena of waking experience are no less devoid of inherent, objective reality than are dreams. So when Padmasambhava states that phenomena are nonexistent—not really there—he means that phenomena don't exist by their own nature, either subjectively or objectively. In other words, phenomena exist interdependently—their appearance to our consciousness depends on a multitude of factors rather than on their having an independent reality from their own side, so to speak. The fact that phenomena appear to our minds and that we give them conventional labels—cloud, cup, Colorado—does not mean they are ultimately real.

Although we usually apply it selectively, the notion of interdependence is not at all foreign to our thinking. Take a "tennis match." The validity of this term depends upon there being at least two opposing players, a tennis court, a net, the racquets, the tennis ball, and the rules of the game. It also depends on the players understanding the game and being physically equipped and in good enough health to play. If any of these interdependent factors is missing, you cannot have a tennis match as it is normally understood.

From the standpoint of Buddhist philosophy, all conditioned phenomena require three things for their existence: (1) prior causes and conditions (such as the parents who were the causes of the birth of the tennis players, or all of the work and planning that went into the construction of the tennis court and the manufacture of the racquets and balls); (2) the components and attributes of the phenomenon itself (the collection of players, court, ball, racquets, the rules of the game, and knowledge brought together to create a game of tennis, etc.); and (3) the conceptual designation that identifies the phenomena possessing these components and attributes (our labeling this collection of objects and events as a "tennis match"). Seen in this manner, a "tennis match" is merely a label, an abstraction. You can observe a tennis match, but you cannot find some independent object that is a tennis match. That is not its nature. It is a conventional phenomenon—we label it by convention, but there is no ultimate, absolute, *tennis-match-thing* to be found.

We can find many similar examples, but when Padmasambhava or other Buddhists speak of "phenomena" and call them nonexistent, they refer to everything we experience with our ordinary modes of perception.[1] Phenomena are traditionally parsed into two domains: the personal self (the "inner") and everything else—the outside world. Normally we assume that our personal selves and the contents of the outside world really exist as independent entities. We assume that when we close our eyes the outside world does not disappear until we open them again, and based on that and other "proofs," the outside world exists in total independence of anyone perceiving it. And we certainly believe that we, too, are absolutely real. When we talk about "my body," "my beliefs," "my house," and "my spouse," we imagine that the person who possesses all of these things is some real "I."

However, if we carefully scrutinize this situation, we will discover that both the personal self and the outside world are, in the sense that Padmasambhava is using the term, nonexistent. Recall that emptiness corresponds to a "not finding" of something you are looking for. If we look for an absolutely real, independent, freestanding personal self, what do we find? Who or what is this self? If you point to your body, well that is designated "body," not "self." We usually think of ourselves as more than our body, so we may say that either the self is *in the body* or the self is the *owner* of the body (as in the common phrase "my body"). But if the self is in the body, just where in the body is it? If you point to your chest and say, "it's in my heart," you can be sure that no heart surgeon has ever seen a self there while operating. And if you say that your self is in your brain—the assumed center of thinking and the apparently centralized space situated between your main sensory organs—no brain surgeon has ever seen a self there, either.

You might retort by saying that this is a simplistic view of the self and that we really exist as something more complex and sophisticated—some kind of pattern or collection of body parts and neuronally produced thoughts, memories, and emotions. But by asserting this idea we have come back to the Buddhist idea of interdependence. Prior causes and conditions (your parents, the planet earth, etc.) contributed to the creation of your body; the components and attributes of mind and body (thoughts, emotions, and physical activities) provide the collection that is the basis of designation of the self who possesses these components and attributes—*my* thoughts and opinions, *my* body, *my* skill as a tennis player, and so forth. The "me" of "my body" is a mere designation—a label. Over millennia, Buddhist philosophers have searched systematically and thoroughly for evidence of an absolute personal self. None has been found. Buddhist contemplatives train for many years searching for this self to see whether there is any experiential evidence for its existence.

Using the same analysis we discover that objects in the outside world, large and small, are also nonexistent in the sense in which Padmasambhava uses the term. Take the "atom." The word originated with the ancient Greeks. Democritus (fourth century B.C.E.) proposed the atom as the smallest particle of matter and the building block of the material universe. Science much later discovered experimentally that the atom was composed of "subatomic particles," and these particles were then assumed to be the real building blocks of the universe—the atoms of the atom. But further experiments, especially beginning in 1900 with the advent of quantum physics, showed that the nature and existence of these particles depended in part on the human thinking that theorized their existence and determined how they were to be measured. For example, a subatomic particle such as an electron can appear as a particle in one type of experiment and as a wave in another. It is the mind of the scientist that designs these experiments, these methods of measurement. But particles and waves are entirely different phenomena—so what does this say about the electron itself? Does it exist? And if so—how? As the pioneering physicist Werner Heisenberg said: "What we observe is not nature in itself but nature exposed to our method of questioning."

The quirkiness of the electron is no single, isolated case. Mainstream physics now accepts that the basic components of the material universe have a nebulous, dreamlike quality. So "atom" becomes, like the personal self, an interdependent entity relying upon prior causes and conditions, components and attributes of the observed phenomena, and most significantly, conceptual designation—labeling, measuring, and experimentation that involves a growing list of subatomic particles and their often-bewildering behaviors. And if the subatomic particles of the atom are not ultimates, if they have no absolute existence, then the objective reality of all the matter supposedly composed of atoms—the whole universe—is thrown into doubt.

But we needn't base our understanding of the nonexistence of the universe on the complexities of modern physics. We can take any common object and arrive at the same conclusion. We made a cursory examination of a teacup in the previous chapter. This time let's look in more detail at another common object—a pencil, for instance. Is a pencil real? Does it exist from its own side as a pencil or is it just a label we apply to a collection? We attach this label to a thin, tubular object made of wood with a graphite center. Usually there is an eraser at one end. As the pencil is used it becomes smaller and smaller. And the eraser gets used up too, often disappearing entirely. It may get to the point where its functional identity—"a writing instrument"—no longer exists. When we ask for a pencil and are handed a stub, we may cry out, "This isn't a pencil! Give me something I can write with." Has its "pencil-ness" evaporated? Where did it go? We could also say that what we call a pencil is merely a short moment in the long history of some wood and minerals. Previously the pencil was a part of a tree and some graphite in the ground as coal, some metal not yet mined and refined, and some rubber in a rubber tree or a synthetic rubber substitute that may come from oil deep within the earth. Later on, the collection, momentarily labeled a "pencil," will disintegrate into dust, fungi, minerals, gases.

The tree, coal, metal, and so on—along with the whole process of the pencil's history and manufacture—constitute the pencil's prior causes and conditions. Its components and attributes are the collection of materials comprising the pencil and its utility as a writing instrument. And it is conceptually designated a "pencil"—an object possessing those components and attributes. But, of course, there is really nothing there that *possesses* these. The wood and graphite and so forth possess nothing. The pencil exists only to the mind that labels and apprehends this object as such. If future civilizations dug up a nice, sharp-pointed pencil, they might designate it as a weapon. So pencils, and all other physical objects, are nonexistent—empty of inherent existence. Their only existence is a conventional, interdependent one; they depend on a collection of other elements being brought together and designated—labeled—by a mind. Furthermore, we cannot retreat to the components of objects and say that since *they* are real, what they constitute must be real. Wood is a collection of cellulose fibers and chemicals comprised of molecules that can be further analyzed down to the subatomic level—which, as we've seen, has only a tentative existence. The same of course goes for graphite, metal, and rubber. At this point we may start to envision "reality" as something far less substantial than we normally assume. Phenomena—inner and outer—seem to be magically called into existence by their labels.

It is in this sense that Padmasambhava calls phenomena nonexistent. Yet even though they are not real, appearances arise and are established, designated, and apprehended as various things. This parallels the way dream phenomena appear to be real to the deluded, nonlucid dreamer, and are seen to be nonexistent once the dreamer either becomes lucid or awakens. Lucid dreaming beckons us to awaken within our nocturnal dreams— to become aware that the dreamed persona that we think is us, along with all other dream phenomena, are illusory. Dream yoga asks us to go further, to awaken to the true nature of an analogous situation that we mistakenly call "waking reality."

THE PROCESS OF DELUSION

Padmasambhava continues his preamble to the instructions on daytime dream yoga: "That which is impermanent is grasped as permanent, and that which is not truly existent is grasped as truly existent." In other words, we reify—we make real to ourselves that which is not real. This could be called the first, the primordial dream sign of Buddhism: *If you are reifying, you are dreaming.* However, if you awaken to this process—see how you are creating the illusion of permanent, truly existent phenomena—you are on the path to seeing things as they are, to enlightenment. The emphasis here is on discovering the process through which we delude ourselves.

Whenever craving or hostility well up within us, it can be very interesting to observe it, watch it arise, watch the object for which there is attachment or hostility, and then ask ourselves: "How does this object—a person, place, thing, situation, whatever it may be—appear to the mind's eye, how am I apprehending it?" See whether it is the case that you are apprehending it as if it were something existing in and of itself—taken out of context by its own apparent self-nature. At that moment, is this the target, the focus of your mind—this "real" object? And if it is, recognize you are dreaming. Because that target doesn't exist in the way you have apprehended it. You are mesmerized by your own assumptions about the object. Your focus is narrow, essentially an invention. The technical term for this in Buddhism is *grasping.*

This kind of delusion is common both in dreams and in waking reality. An example is how we often decontextualize people who appear to us either when dreaming or in daytime situations. We see someone, observe their behavior, perhaps interact with them, and come away with the opinion that this person is "smart," "attractive," "stupid," "ugly," or "a jerk." Taking the last attribute, whether the person appears in a dream or during daytime, he or she seems to us to be a jerk from his or her own side. The person appears permeated with the qualities of "jerk-ness"—inherent characteristics that are merely presented to us and we passively recognize them. It's a case of judging the book by its cover.

But we haven't read the book. If we analyze just a little we discover that the true context of this person is immensely complex. For example, this person may have parents who think he or she is not a jerk but is an adorable person. Many other people may not call this person a jerk. The person you perceive as a jerk probably does not conceive of him- or herself as a jerk. And if you got to know this person, over time even the qualities you consider jerky might be apprehended in a different way. (Conversely, there are no doubt people out there who think that *you* are a jerk—something to which you probably would not agree.)

Obviously, when we awaken from a nonlucid dream about a jerk, the reality of that situation vanishes like smoke. Since the dreamed person was nonexistent, the label "jerk" was also imaginary. When we view people so narrowly, whether in dreams or waking reality, we invariably decontextualize—placing absolute labels where no absolutes exist. The true context for all persons and objects is interdependence. The condition of dreaming, whether it be in the night or in daytime, subsumes a form of ignorance where we can easily misconstrue appearances. Dreaming invites us to become deluded. We can either go with the flow or wake up—check it right there and realize that although the object as we perceive it appears to be real from its own side, that appearance is illusory.

In terms of our normal mode of understanding reality, analyzing phenomena in this way turns everything on its head. But even if we are, at this point, thoroughly convinced that "all phenomena are nonexistent," our present understanding is only conceptual. In Tibetan Buddhism, conceptual understanding is likened to a patch on clothing that sooner or later falls away. It is the habituation of the practice of daytime dream yoga that will allow our understanding to deepen and prepare us for an awakening that encompasses both the day and the night. To quote Chagdud Tulku Rinpoche—one of the most prominent Tibetan lamas who taught in the West—"All dream yoga is based on the one-pointedness one can maintain on the illusoriness of experience by day."[2]

THE PRACTICE OF ILLUSORY BODY

"Consider," continues Padmasambhava, "that since all these things, which are without permanence, stability, or immutability, have no inherent nature, they are like illusions." What are illusions like? They seem to exist, but they're not really there where they appear. We have already examined our personal self, the atom, the "jerk," and a common object—the pencil. And perhaps you can agree that under analysis these objects have an illusory quality: they appear to exist independently, from their own side, but they don't. We assume they exist, but we cannot pin them down with any exactitude. We have the idea of a personal self in our minds, but phenomenologically—that is, in terms of our direct experience—we haven't encountered an independent entity that matches our conception of any of these objects. Padmasambhava now asks us to see waking reality in a new way: from moment to moment, situation to situation, person to person, view all that arises as being not permanent, not immutable, not inherently existent but rather to be appearing like illusions, appearing like a dream.

If this sounds like a nutty thing to do—to say, "This is an illusion" to everything that arises in your experience—modern neuroscience, just like physics, supports this affirmation. All of the information that appears to our senses seems to come from "out there." Earlier we touched on the fact that the colors we perceive in the outside world do not actually exist objectively, independent of perception. The molecules that make up material objects do not have color. The photons that strike our retinas are colorless, and the neurons in the visual cortex don't take on the colors that we perceive. The colors we perceive therefore do not exist in physical space—not in the objects, not in the space between our sense organs and those objects, and not in the brain. From a Buddhist point of view, colors and all other appearances to our physical senses and to mental perception all arise from the substrate. The cooperative conditions of learning, memory, imagination, along with the electrochemical processes that occur in the optic nerve, must combine to produce the subjective appearance we call "red." Red roses are not red unto themselves, just waiting for us to passively perceive them. According to the prominent neurologist Antonio Damasio, "There is no picture of the object being transferred from the object to the retina and from the retina to the brain."[3] And it may well be that other kinds of retinas, optic nerves, visual cortexes, and conditioned minds—such as those of bees, or bats, or bears—give rise to a completely different experience of what we call a red rose. Which is the "real" red rose? There is none. The red rose is an illusion. From the modern neuroscientific perspective, the same is true for the objects of the other senses. So when we close our eyes, the world—in the unique form in which we view it—*does* disappear. Something is seen by others, but it isn't precisely what we see. And if those others are of other species, it may be something completely different.

In the Dhammapada, the Buddha says, "Mind precedes all phenomena." We may interpret the mind he refers to as the substrate consciousness, the continuum of awareness filled with latent tendencies, impressions, memories, habitual modes of perception, and so forth. Mind precedes phenomena in the sense that phenomena are conditioned by the substrate consciousness. It filters all, or practically all, that we perceive. When we awaken from sleep, it is said that the nightscape dissolves into the substrate. And when we fall asleep, likewise the dayscape dissolves into the same space. Note that it is appearances—not photons or sound waves—that dissolve into the substrate. Photons, sound waves, and the like are theoretical entities of science that we cannot perceive directly, so they exist relative to the systems of measurement by which they are detected and relative to the minds that conceive them. And as is demonstrated by our dreams, the substrate is a dynamo, creating one environment after another. The entire world of subjects and objects in which we are embedded—which we call "life,"

and which Buddhism calls samsara—arises out of the entangle-
ment, the complex conglomeration of mutual substrates.

We note again what Stephen LaBerge says so astutely: "Dream
consciousness is waking consciousness without physical constraints. Waking consciousness is dream consciousness with
physical constraints." The crux of the matter is: What are physical constraints? What is their nature? Lucid dream researchers,
with their scientific orientation, accept them as being real. Or if
they are not ultimately real, they are at least of another nature
from the phenomena of nocturnal dreaming—"more real" than
our dreams. But Padmasambhava, and the Vajrayana Buddhist
world that he represents, see all phenomena as dreamlike—
empty of fixed, ultimate qualities. Certain Buddhist adepts (and
those from other traditions) occasionally demonstrate this fact
in public. Some tertöns, we are told, can reach into solid rock as
if it were putty and pull out texts and sacred objects. Padmasambhava has left his footprints in solid rock. Modern-day Tibetan lamas have left foot- and handprints in rock and passed
wooden staves through the same material. These "miracles" are
sometimes performed before large numbers of people, those
who perform them altering waking reality in much the same
way as lucid dreamers alter dream reality. The point is not to
show off "esoteric powers" but to instill faith that the dream
world may extend beyond the night to what we consider "hard
reality."[4] But to make our conceptual understanding of the
"nonexistence of phenomena" a reality in our lives, we must do
what these extraordinary beings have done: practice.

THE PRACTICE

Padmasambhava gives us the essential, specific instruction for
daytime dream yoga practice: "At this time, powerfully imagine
that your environment, city, house, companions, conversation,
and all activities are a dream; and even say out loud, 'This is a
dream.' Continually imagine that this is just a dream." Another

Tibetan Buddhist teaching on daytime dream yoga[5] elaborates on these instructions, encouraging the student to "establish single-pointed meditative equipoise in the awareness, 'I have fallen asleep. This appearance is a dream. It is an illusion.'" Furthermore, you are to "place your awareness in a nonconceptual sphere, without focusing it anywhere. Then direct your mind to all the appearances of yourself and others, and think, 'All these are just appearances. They are not real.' By continually practicing in that way, at all times during and after formal meditation, appearances will always seem devoid of true existence and of fear." Now it becomes clear why the resolve and concentration derived from the practice of shamatha is essential for the successful practice of daytime dream yoga.

This practice points directly to the key difference between the daytime practices of lucid dreaming and those of dream yoga. If in daytime you complete a dozen state checks, and ten times in a row your digital clock gives you the same answer when you glance away and look back—in terms of lucid dreaming you can be 99 percent sure that you are not dreaming. And yet Padmasambhava suggests that even so, even though you are sure you are "awake," you should tell yourself you are dreaming. Padmasambhava is not inviting us to practice a self-induced illusion. He is asking us to pull the rug out from under our habitual perspective on what we are experiencing. He is reframing what it means to be awake and making this the focus of daytime practice.

Returning to the example of a nonlucid dream: as long as you are operating from the assumption that you are the person in the dream—the dreamed persona—you are stuck in that point of view. If that's who you think you really are, you've sealed the nonlucidity of your dream. You are locked into your illusory role. If a companion were to notice you are dreaming—perhaps by seeing that you are tossing and turning and mumbling and your eyes display rapid eye movement—he might whisper into your ear, "You are dreaming."[6] And just like this companion,

Padmasambhava is asking you to view the dream not from the perspective of the deluded dream persona but, figuratively speaking, from that of the dreamer asleep in bed. He is suggesting that you view waking reality from the perspective of buddha-nature. The Buddha was once asked, "Are you a god, a celestial being, a spirit, or a man?" He replied, none of the above, "I am awake."[7]

From the Dzogchen perspective, Padmasambhava's instruction is that we attempt to see reality as it really is. We are to view not only the outside world but our own bodies as dream phenomena. As a preparation for nighttime dream yoga we practice the instructions on illusory body—to view one's body as simply a matrix of illusions. The body and its constituents are seen as no more substantial than a reflection in a mirror.[8] Since we have not arrived yet at primordial consciousness, we use the power of imagination. So you "powerfully imagine" being completely lucid in the waking state. Doing so is a big step toward actually becoming lucid. By placing the imagination on something for which the fit is perfect—you do happen to be dreaming after all—by pretending to see things as they really are, you have created a template that matches reality. Then your imagination may open up, break down the barriers that are preventing you from seeing what is already there—that you are dreaming. And from a Buddhist perspective, from the perspective of pristine awareness, primordial consciousness, waking reality is not just "dream*like*," it *is* a dream. So now we try to truly wake up in what we normally and erroneously call the waking state.

PRIMORDIAL CONSCIOUSNESS

In the nighttime practice of lucid dreaming, when we are able say in the midst of a dream, "I am dreaming," the reference for "I" emerges from the substrate consciousness. That is its locus. This is the ordinary, conventional "I." What is the referent for "I" when we say—authentically, with full understanding—"I am dreaming," in the practice of daytime dream yoga? Who or what is dreaming, is delusional about waking reality? This waking reality is being dreamed by primordial consciousness. This is one reason that it is said in Vajrayana that all visual appearances are the body of the deity, all sounds the speech of the deity, and all thoughts are the mind of the deity. The deity, of course, is fully enlightened—is a manifestation of enlightened mind. And in Dzogchen it is said that all beings are already enlightened and the billionfold universe is a buddha realm. In essence we are not ordinary sentient beings but enlightened beings that fail to recognize the fact. This follows the old Tibetan aphorism, "Although the sun is always shining, adventitious clouds hide it from our view."

The reality of primordial consciousness, or pristine awareness, is of course something that can be known. But it is not known just by carefully observing appearances, nor by the power of logic, intellect, investigation, and so forth. You could say that it can be known by the power of *faith*—but that can lead us into semantic difficulties. It's a knowing that is not simply empirical knowing by way of the senses, not a knowing by way of inference, but a knowing that is immediate, that is unmediated, nonconceptual—*intuitive*. The experience is one of pristine awareness knowing itself.

I would summarize Padmasambhava's quintessential instruction for daytime dream yoga in this way: with the power of your intuition and imagination keep on dropping back into the perspective from which it is true to say, "This is a dream." Sustain that. That will gradually break down the barriers between your normal dualistic mind and pristine awareness. So daytime dream yoga is moved by the power of intuition and sustained by the power of mindfulness.

7

Nighttime Dream Yoga

MOTIVATION

"When you go to bed in the evening," says Padmasambhava, "cultivate bodhichitta, thinking, 'For the sake of all sentient beings throughout space, I shall practice the illusion-like samadhi [dream yoga], and I shall achieve perfect buddhahood. For that purpose I shall train in dreaming.'" This gives us our bearings. What would be the most meaningful motivation for training in dream yoga? Try this one on for size: to benefit all beings by bringing them to enlightenment. In the context of Vajrayana and Dzogchen there is only one suitable motivation and that is bodhichitta. The aspiration is the highest and the words are emphatic: "I shall achieve perfect buddhahood." We are not saying, "Oh, I'll give it my best shot and I hope I don't die first."

Such a high motivation brings with it some far-reaching questions. Can you really dedicate yourself to achieving bodhichitta—with all that it implies—while maintaining the working assumption that when you die all bets are off? I don't know how that can possibly be realistic unless you are almost there—almost awakened when you begin this practice—or unless you downgrade bodhichitta to the mere catch phrase, "may everybody be happy." It would seem that the working hypothesis of reincarnation—that we can propel ourselves to continue this practice, this work, in future lifetimes if need be—would be very helpful if not essential for us to seriously make the assertion that Padmasambhava asks us to make.

This brings to mind the true story of my teacher Gen Lamrimpa, who arrived in India as a penniless monk in the 1960s, soon after the Communist Chinese had invaded Tibet and begun their brutal repression of Buddhism. He landed in a small town called Dehradun in northern India, in the foothills of the Himalayas. There he discovered that among the Tibetan refugees in this village were a number of highly accomplished teachers and adepts. Although many of them had barely escaped with their lives, had few possessions, and were newly exiled from their homeland, from the viewpoint of spiritual practice, here was a unique gathering of individuals—a treasure for a sincere practitioner of Dharma.

But not only was Gen Lamrimpa penniless, there was no place for him to live and practice. Even the caves around the village were filled up with yogis—"no vacancy!" So Gen Lamrimpa found not a cave but an overhanging rock. Now this is an area where it rains heavily throughout much of the year, so his new home didn't provide much in the way of shelter. But there under his rock he sat down to practice. He discovered that the U.S. government was giving Tibetan refugees a bag of flour each month, and that was pretty much all he ate. For three or four years that was his situation: an overhanging rock and a bag of flour. Later on he told me that these were some of the happiest days of his life. So the question arises: would a person do what Gen Lamrinmpa did without a worldview that made that an immensely meaningful enterprise—one that would be meaningful not only for this lifetime but in future lives, so that all the time spent in arduous practice would carry over and any task unfinished in this life would be continued in the next?

If one did not have such a worldview and believed that at the end of this life there is annihilation, that would be like a businessman being told that he could spend his time and energy developing his business, but that at any moment—willy-nilly—he might go bankrupt. How much drive would you have toward achieving your goal if that were your working hypothesis (as opposed to pouring your heart and soul into a business knowing that it would benefit your children and grandchildren)? So seriously taking on bodhichitta as your motivation for dream yoga practice has significant ramifications that you should investigate.

PRACTICE

The instructions continue: "Then as you lie down, rest on your right shoulder, with your head pointed north, your right hand pressed against your cheek, and your left placed upon your thigh. Clearly imagine your body as your personal deity." This position is called the sleeping-lion posture. If you cannot arrange your bed so it is pointing north—or if you are traveling a lot and sleeping mainly in hotels—simply imagine that you are pointing north. That will do. The term "personal deity" is the translation of the Tibetan word *yidam*. This could be a deity such as Vajrasattva, Tara, or Padmasambhava, or it could be your own primary spiritual mentor, your guru. You might imagine yourself as Padmasambhava, the Dalai Lama, Karmapa, or as other great teachers such as Dudjom Rinpoche or Dilgo Kyentse Rinpoche. So use whatever archetypal form or manifestation of the Buddha, symbolically expressing those qualities of buddhahood, most deeply resonate with you, and imagine yourself in that form—imagine your body as your own yidam. (Or you can use as your yidam some other spiritual figure in whom you find inspiration. If you are a Christian you could use Jesus Christ or someone like Saint Francis of Assisi. Inspiring personalities of great spiritual integrity are to be found in all the world's religions as well as within secular contexts.) "If your visualization is not clear," continues Padmasambhava, "establish the pride of thinking, 'I am the personal deity.'"

DEITIES

Deity practice may be considered the heart of Vajrayana Buddhism. The formal practice of meditating on a personal deity is exceedingly complex. In general terms, the practitioner visually memorizes the form of the deity including the deity's apparel, hand implements, and gestures (*mudra*). Each of these has a special significance. For example, the vulture's feather atop Padmasambhava's hat signifies that his view is the highest. His three robes (an inner and outer robe over which is a cape) represent his mastery of the Shravakayana (the vehicle of individual liberation), Mahayana, and Vajrayana; and so on. The practitioner then essentially empties him- or herself of any reference to the ordinary personality and visualizes his or her body as that of the deity. Using "divine pride,"[1] one affirms one's identity with the deity. The outer world is viewed as the *mandala* of the deity, typically containing a palace with four symmetric entrances guarded by protectors, surrounded by auspicious symbols, protective circles, and other figures and symbols. Persons in the outer world are viewed as fully enlightened beings.[2] Ideally all physical forms are recognized as the body of the deity, all sounds as its enlightened speech, all thoughts as its enlightened mind. The entire visualization represents the universe seen as a buddha realm bearing all of the attributes of enlightenment.

It is essential here, as in all deity practice, to cast off your ordinary sense of identity. This is accomplished by first realizing that your normal sense of self is empty—it is constructed and contrived—a house of cards that collapses when examined closely. This can be accomplished using the style of analysis shown earlier that reveals the "nonexistence" of phenomena, coupled with the stable concentration developed in shamatha practice. From that domain of emptiness of inherent existence you arise in the form of the deity while assuming the identity with the deity. Visualizing yourself as your personal deity, imagine that you possess those qualities of perfect enlightenment embodied in your yidam. In doing so you transform yourself and your environment into a template of enlightened awareness.[3]

Padmasambhava's specific instructions for falling asleep suggest that you "imagine that on your pillow your head is resting in the lap of your primary spiritual mentor; and vividly focus your attention on Orgyen Padma [Padmasambhava] at your throat, the size of your thumb joint, with a smiling, lustrous countenance, appearing and yet having no inherent nature." The image that you visualize appears vividly in your throat but is transparent, like a rainbow. Then, "mentally offer the supplication, 'Bless me that I may apprehend the dream-state. Bless me so that I may recognize the dream-state as the dream-state.'" You are recognizing your own Buddha-nature as Padmasambhava at your throat chakra and calling forth to your innermost awareness to bring clarity to your dreams. You are not calling upon some outside power or personality for assistance.

"Lie in the sleeping-lion position, and bring forth a powerful yearning to recognize the dream-state as the dream-state." In a manner very similar to the nighttime practice of lucid dreaming, bring forth a strong resolve, create the strong prospective memory—*Tonight I am totally resolved to recognize the dream state!* "And while so doing, fall asleep without being interrupted by any other thoughts." This is where extensive shamatha practice would be indispensable, enabling you to hold the resolve, the prospective memory, with a quiet, stable mind. "Even if you do not apprehend it at the first try, repeat this many times, and earnestly do it with powerful yearning." Clearly this is a challenging agenda: to fall asleep while visualizing Padmasambhava in your throat chakra, making the resolutions, and holding the visualization, not allowing any static or interference from other extraneous thoughts to interfere.

Normally after going to bed we allow the mind to just dither all over the place for a while, and then fall asleep in a state of semiconscious inner chitchat. So we must train ourselves to calm that obsessive, compulsive, blathering mind and just get some quiet so we can hold this resolve, hold the prospective memory—very relaxed with a quiet mind—and then slip right into sleep.

When you concentrate on one of the chakras, subtle, vital energy converges there. During the waking state the vital energies naturally converge in your head, during dreaming they converge at the throat, and in deep, dreamless sleep they converge in the heart chakra. So if you want to awaken in your dreams, by focusing on the throat chakra you are gathering vital energies in a way that will prepare you to consciously enter the dream state.

For most people, the greatest challenge is to hold this visualization and still fall asleep. This calls for either very subtle attention skills or a mind that is by nature extremely relaxed. In traditional Tibetan culture, calm, relaxed minds were more common. This was a largely rural and nomadic society—the few cities were small and peaceful in comparison to the modern metropolis. Also, from my own experience, it is much easier to practice visualization at high altitudes such as those found throughout Tibet, "the roof of the world." One of my Tibetan teachers, in his youth, spent his summers as a shepherd in alpine pastures. All day long he did nothing other than watch his family's herd as they wandered lazily among the grasses—his only entertainment being a wooden flute. In such a lifestyle it is not so difficult to grow accustomed to having a relaxed and peaceful mind. Again, if your mind is generally agitated—not an uncommon situation for us in the modern world—developing shamatha through dedicated practice would be rewarding not just for accomplishing dream yoga but for enhancing a wide spectrum of activities.

There are simpler alternative visualizations that can be used for direct entry into the dreamscape. You may imagine a red *bindu*—a glowing red pearl of light—in your throat. The white syllable *AH,* which symbolizes emptiness, can be imagined as well. You can use the Tibetan letter for this syllable, the Sanskrit, or the English transliteration "AH." But the essence of this practice is to focus your awareness on the throat chakra, visualize it there—give it form. By doing so you are crystallizing something, your awareness is taking on a form, you are converging the vital energies there. When you visualize a specific seed syllable or even hear its sound, by bringing in these archetypical forms not only are you channeling vital energy to that chakra, you are configuring that energy so it will be of use for dream yoga. The vital energies will help to bring your waking consciousness down from the head to the throat, leading you as directly as possible from the waking state to dream consciousness, and doing so lucidly. So that is the whole point of this procedure.

If you can generally fall asleep quite easily but you still find that trying to maintain a visualization prevents you from falling asleep, then you might try settling the mind in its natural state as you lie in the sleeping-lion posture and slip into sleep. If you can maintain the clarity of your awareness as you doze off, you may enter the sleep state lucidly. And from there you may emerge knowingly into a dream—lucid from the very beginning. But if you normally find it hard to fall asleep, all the above practices may keep you awake. In that case, gently attend to the sensations of your breath and get a good night's sleep. After all, if you can't fall asleep, you can't dream, in which case dream yoga is out of the question!

HINDRANCES

But what can you do if, after a period of dedicated practice to dream yoga, you find yourself stymied, unable to access the dream world lucidly? "If the dream is not apprehended . . . there may be an infraction of your tantric pledges, so apply yourself to going for refuge, cultivating bodhichitta, restoring [your vows] through confession, the one-hundred-syllable mantra [of the deity Vajrasattva],[4] the *ganacakra* offering,[5] avoiding contamination, and meditating in the previous way." Those who have taken tantric pledges (Sanskrit, *samaya*), usually given by the teacher when you receive a tantric empowerment, should investigate to see if any of these vows have been broken. If so, this may result in a blockage that prevents you from progressing in this practice. The blockage can be cleared by an appropriate purification practice such as those mentioned above. If you are not a practitioner of Vajrayana, look to see if you are maintaining a high ethical standard in your dealings with yourself and others. If not, this may be producing a negative influence on your practice and impair the tranquility of mind necessary for successful meditation practice.

Although some of the instructions for nighttime dream yoga may seem daunting, we can take a more practical approach to get ourselves off the ground. First, recognize the dream. Use anything that helps—the techniques elucidated by Padmasambhava above or any of the methods from modern lucid dreaming that work for you. The whole point is to simply become lucid in the dream so that you have a basis for whatever dream-yoga activities you choose to enact. Next, in order to practice easily and effectively, maintain the stability and vividness of your recognition that you are dreaming, and also maintain the stability and vividness of the dream itself. How deeply have you fathomed the dream state as the dream state in terms of vividness? There is a whole continuum of degrees of lucidity. Have you cognized it so clearly that you could walk up to what appears to be a granite wall in a dream and go right through it? Here once more we note the relevance of shamatha to dream yoga because the stability and vividness in the dream will be precisely that of your mind before you fell asleep. As long as you cultivate stability and vividness of attention through shamatha, you can simply carry that over into your dream yoga practice and things will go more smoothly. That's why Padmasambhava taught shamatha first and dream yoga afterward.

THE CORE PRACTICES OF EMANATION AND TRANSFORMATION

The essential practices of dream yoga employ lucidity while dreaming to develop a direct understanding of the nature of phenomena. Padmasambhava says, "While apprehending the dream state, consider, 'Since this is now a dream body it can be transformed in any way.' Whatever arises in a dream, be they demonic apparitions, monkeys, people, dogs, and so on, meditatively transform them into your personal deity. Practice multiplying them by emanation and changing them into anything you like."

You could call this the "sorcerer phase" of dream yoga. You are in the dream, you know that you are dreaming, you are maintaining the continuity and clarity of the dream itself and the continuity of your awareness of dreaming. Knowing that all appearances are just emanations of the substrate—that there's nothing there substantial from its own side subjectively or objectively—you can simply start modifying whatever you like within the dream. Some things, like flying, are easy and very malleable. By now you have probably logged plenty of flight time. At this stage, the classic procedure is to transform the one into many and the many into one. Try that with any object that appears, including yourself. If you see a cocker spaniel in your dream, create a dozen. If you see a flock of pigeons, reduce them to a single bird.

Next shift the size of objects—small into big and big into small. Turn a planet that fills your visual field into the same object the size of a golf ball. Magnify an ant to the size of a mountain. Then shift the shape and identity of objects. Turn the cocker spaniel into a crocodile, and then back again. Transform yourself into a bird, a mountain, or a wristwatch. Fashion yourself into a disembodied spirit and then into a field of flowers. My teacher Gyatrul Rinpoche calls this the practice of "moving gross and subtle appearances of sentient beings and the environment back and forth," suggesting you change objects "in any way that you like," including that you "transform the peaceful into the wrathful and the wrathful into the peaceful." So anything goes.

At first you will encounter certain emanations and transformations that are resistant to your will, difficult to perform. In these instances you must exert yourself because there is something in the lucid dream that you are still reifying; there appears to be some objective resistance, something is not malleable to the play of your own awareness. So you must work on it until you get it completely free. You must realize not only conceptually but also experientially that dream phenomena are entirely fluid. Nothing that appears in the dream is independent of your consciousness. Gradually you come to know this through having performed these experiments. This is hands-on learning. The tendency to reify stops not because you have suppressed it but because you know these phenomena are unreal through your own experience—that is the overarching reason you are practicing dream yoga. Although it can be a lot of fun to play with these things, the point of these exercises is to thoroughly saturate your understanding with the knowledge that dream phenomena have no inherent existence from their own side.

YOUR WORST NIGHTMARE

Do not be surprised if after a time the deep practice of dream yoga occasionally brings up unpleasant experiences. We are exploring the substrate, which contains the good, the bad, and the ugly of our experience of not only this life but countless past lives. If we had been angelic in all of those lives—our actions always positive and virtuous, generating only positive karma—we would be enlightened by now. So we must deal with some of the gnarly aspects of our being. One form of this, which appears both in dream yoga and in deep shamatha practice, is *nyam,* Tibetan for "meditative experience." Of course there is an extraordinarily wide range of such experiences. A nyam is an anomalous, transient psychological and/or somatic experience that is catalyzed by proper meditation. So it is anomalous—something out of the ordinary. It's transient—it probably doesn't last more than a few hours or at the most a couple of days. It may manifest in the body as nausea, as vertigo, as bliss, all kinds of somatic experiences, or, psychologically, as depression, paranoia, burgeoning faith, reverence, tears, sadness, and so on. Note that it is catalyzed by *proper* meditation practices and is a sign of progress, to be distinguished from experiences triggered by wrong-headed meditative practice.

The more intense the practice, the better it is to have on call a qualified meditation teacher. When nyam arise, be sensible: Ask yourself, "Could this be a medical condition?" If the answer is "maybe," go to a doctor. When you are sure it is nyam, just let it be. Simply be present with it without generating hope or fear. If it is nyam it will just pass on through. Genuine nyam are a good sign—you are practicing well and correctly—and passing through these phases properly is a process of purification.

The deepest levels of the practice of transformation and emanation may catalyze the nyam of fears. For some object to evoke fear in the mind there must be a dense, intractable reification taking place. The object is grasped as absolutely threatening. "Apprehend the dream-state and go to the bank of a great river," says Padmasambhava. "Consider, 'Since I am a mental body in a dream, there is nothing for the river to carry away.' By jumping into the river you will be carried away by a current of bliss and emptiness." Because the practices of dream yoga (and of shamatha) dredge down deep into the substrate consciousness, sooner or later your worst nightmare will come to the surface. Echoing Padmasambhava's words, the Tibetan lama Tsongkapa said, "whenever anything of a threatening or traumatic nature occurs in a dream, such as drowning in water or being burned by fire, recognize the dream as a dream and . . . make yourself jump or fall into the water or fire in the dream."[6] Consider bringing lucidity to the following nightmare as a candidate for a worst fear:

> I am floating in the dark, viscous waters of a swamp. Suddenly I notice two hungry eyes above the surface of the water moving toward me. I am about to become a meal for this frightening beast. I know that I am dreaming. I don't exist, the crocodile doesn't exist, the whole environment is a mental fabrication. I could easily escape by flying to the moon or just transform the croc into a cuddly cocker spaniel. But I don't. I let him come on, open his gaping jaws, show his razor-sharp teeth, and crunch down on my tender, helpless body. (There is no pain, of course, because my dream body has no nerve endings and the crocodile's teeth are insubstantial.) And when he is done I reconstitute myself, turn to the crocodile, and ask, "Would you like another course?" And I let him do it again.

This is the final exam for this phase of practice—to allow your worst nightmare to take place knowing perfectly well it is an illusion. "At first," says Padmasambhava, "because of the clinging of self-grasping, you won't dare [to jump into the fire, etc.], but that won't happen once you have grown accustomed to it. Similarly, by seeing through all things such as fire, precipices, and carnivorous animals, all fears will arise as samadhi." The crucial preparation for all of that is training in daytime appearances and the illusory body and powerfully anticipating the dream state.

BREAKING THROUGH TO PRIMORDIAL CONSCIOUSNESS

In *Natural Liberation*, Padmasambhava presents an advanced practice for recognizing pristine awareness in the dream state. Utilizing this, students who have already fully accomplished shamatha and *vipashyana*[7] may be able dwell in *rigpa*, or pristine awareness, in the dream state. However, a person lacking these prerequisites may also attain glimpses of primordial consciousness by allowing awareness to descend into the substrate consciousness, using the methods presented in chapter 4 (closing one's eyes during a lucid dream, falling asleep while meditating on a visualization at the heart chakra, and practicing awareness of awareness). When you release the dream but sustain your lucidity and your awareness dissolves from the psyche of the dream consciousness into the substrate consciousness, obviously that is an opportunity for directly realizing the substrate consciousness. But you may, in that state, practice Dzogchen in the lucid dreamless state. And by releasing all grasping in this panoramic, 360-degree open awareness, your awareness may break through the substrate consciousness and be realized as pristine awareness. It is clear from some of the earliest teachings by Prahevajra on the Dzogchen practice of *trekchö*, of "breakthrough,"[8] what you are actually breaking through is your substrate consciousness.[9]

The authentic practice of Dzogchen, however, entails much more than simply resting in "choiceless awareness" or "open presence." These practices are not even genuine shamatha practices, for shamatha always involves selective attention, not openness to all appearances. Moreover, if you're still attending to sensory appearances, your mind will never withdraw into the substrate consciousness, so you'll never achieve shamatha. Choiceless awareness and open presence are also not really vipashyana practices, for true vipashyana always involves some degree of inquiry, which those practices lack. And finally neither of those two practices by themselves constitute Dzogchen meditation, for genuine Dzogchen involves a thorough immersion into the view, meditation, and way of life of Dzogchen. Without coming to view reality from the perspective of pristine awareness, open presence is nothing more than resting in one's ordinary, dualistic mind. The classic sequence of practice in the Dzogchen tradition consists of settling the mind in the substrate consciousness through the practice of shamatha, exploring the ultimate nature of the mind through the practice of vipashyana, and finally penetrating through the conventional mind, namely the substrate consciousness, to pristine awareness through the practice of *trekchö* meditation.

So, with the substrate consciousness as a platform, one may break through to pristine awareness. Some appearances that arise in the dream may be mere artifacts emerging from your substrate, but from the Dzogchen perspective you may actually encounter a buddha, and you may receive teachings directly from such a being. So for those whose practice is immersed in Vajrayana, there is the possibility of traveling to buddhafields, encountering buddhas, and receiving teachings.

Throughout Buddhist history many instances of this have been recorded. For advanced practitioners—of whom there are many, especially in Asia—it is almost a commonplace. One of the most famous examples is the Dzogchen adept Jigme Lingpa (1730–1798) who received extensive transmissions and teachings in dreams from Longchen Rabjam (1308–1364), even though more than four centuries separate their lifetimes. Longchen Rabjam himself had received numerous teachings and transmissions directly through dreams and visions. But here is a more recent example: I once visited the English nun, Tenzin Palmo, who is one of the best Western practitioners of Tibetan Buddhism out there.[10] She lived in a cave at an altitude of fifteen thousand feet in complete isolation for many years. At the time I met her she was collecting all her provisions, food and firewood, to start a continuous three-year retreat.

I asked her, given that she would be snowed-in from November to May, what happens in February when she might have some important practice question but no way to ask a teacher. She replied, "It's easy, I pray to my lama and then he appears in my dream and I get all my answers that way." One of the perks of samadhi is that the clarity of awareness naturally flows into the dream state. People who have attained the one-pointed samadhi that is the fruit of accomplishing shamatha start to have lucid dreams even with no specific dream training at all.

Although remembering past lives may involve deeply accessing the substrate consciousness, *siddhis* such as clairvoyance (seeing things occurring at a great distance), clairaudience (hearing things at a great distance), premonitions, and other types of "extrasensory perception" suggest access to primordial consciousness, where time and space are not barriers to knowledge. Again, deep meditation practices such as dream yoga may allow one occasional access to these paranormal perceptions. Recall the example given earlier, of some yogis I lived with up above Dharamsala, India, in 1980. These were practitioners who had been up there for ten, twenty, thirty years, so their minds had become quite transparent and subtle. A number of them discovered that precognition started to arise frequently. They believed there was no way that it could have been chance or coincidence. Once in a while, completely unpredictably every three or four weeks, a villager would hike up to where the yogis were to leave a small offering. Or if one of the yogis was not on strict retreat, a villager might come to ask a few questions during lunchtime. The yogis found that frequently the night before a villager would arrive, one of them would have a dream of the particular person who would visit. They were getting glimpses into short-term precognition.

In a more recent case, a Tibetan Buddhist teacher, living at his monastery in relative isolation at about sixteen thousand feet in the Himalayas, became instantly aware of the unexpected death of one of his American students in Colorado. The stepson of this student was at this time practicing with this teacher in Tibet, and the teacher informed him of his stepfather's passing, telling him he should head back home. Shortly afterward a telephone call came from Colorado confirming the facts and requesting the young man's return.

A final point regarding these paranormal abilities: In 1992 the Dalai Lama made reference to a practice that was possible for those who are very accomplished yogis and already quite advanced in the practice of dream yoga. With that as a basis, one may enter into something that is explicitly a Vajrayana dream-yoga practice and—this really stretches the imagination—one may develop what the Dalai Lama referred to as the *special dream body.* Here one gains mastery over the subtle energies in the body. You shape them, crafting them as a potter forms a pot, refining and shaping and directing the subtle energies with the power of your samadhi. You're not just working with the substrate, which is intangible and immaterial, you are using the power of your samadhi to create an ethereal body composed of energy. That energy is *prana.* Once you have created this pranic body while meditating within the dream state, you project it, send it out into the intersubjective world, into "ordinary reality."

This is truly an out-of-the-body experience, and what you send out is not some immaterial ghostly emanation. Nor is it the intuitional power of clairvoyance. Rather, you are actually projecting something physical that is imbued with your awareness and that is localized (in the sense of something being *here* versus *there*). It is physical on a very subtle level, and with it you can leave your body and witness things in intersubjective reality that other people see with normal perception. The yogi practicing this technique can state, "I projected my special dream body to such and such a place—five miles away—and this is what I saw." People five miles away can confirm this, saying, "Yes, I saw the same thing." And this is not limited as to distance. One can travel great distances as easily as short ones, and one moves at the speed of thought. This body can even be sent to a pure land, a buddhafield. So this indeed stretches the imagination. Maybe it's true and maybe it's not. The only way to know for sure would be to run the experiment—and that would be a big experiment.

PART THREE

Bringing It All Together

8

Putting Your Dreams to Work

PREVIOUSLY I INTRODUCED the idea of creating dream laboratories. Of course to do so requires that you first gain a certain level of proficiency in lucid dreaming—that you have lucid dreams frequently, that they be of relatively long duration, and that you are able to easily create and manipulate objects and dream environments. If you have reached that plane, you are to be congratulated, because for most of us that takes time and effort.

The sheer excitement and enthusiasm of attaining such abilities can be likened to that of an artist once he or she has reached the professional level. A painter begins with some basic ability to draw or paint, but after much study and practice that person has developed a malleable technique whereby wonderful paintings can be produced with relative ease—works of art that are a vibrant response to a creative imagination. Of course this analogy holds true for any artistic or creative area.

Some of the activities for which you may choose to apply your now considerable skills in lucid dreaming and dream yoga have probably already emerged as you learned these skills. Your choices will come out of the panorama of your interests, activities, and current life challenges, along with options that will appear in the future. Without going into a great deal of depth, this chapter outlines some of the avenues you may wish to explore in dream practice, touched on earlier.

FUN

Although my own emphasis in lucid dreaming and dream yoga has been on developing the spiritual side of life, along with some scientific and philosophical questions that intrigue me, the initial experiences of lucid dreaming are certainly full of fun and excitement. For the hedonist—one who believes that the pursuit of pleasure is the highest good and proper aim of human life— the lucid dreamscape is the ultimate playground. Of course when it comes to pleasures such as eating and sex—or the pursuit of adventure—your imagination is the limit. As Stephen LaBerge says in *Exploring the World of Lucid Dreaming*, "When you are beginning to shape your dreams, wish fulfillment is a natural thing to pursue." But there are also some very useful ways in which the possibilities of wish fulfillment in lucid dreaming can alleviate difficult situations in life over which we have little control.

One of the most capable lucid dreamers I have encountered is a person I mentioned earlier who is confined to a wheelchair by lifelong physical disabilities. During sleep, she makes up for these restrictions by creating a dream life filled with movement and fantastic transformations. Anyone with severe physical limitations could benefit from the practice of lucid dreaming. Imagine the exhilaration, fun, and satisfaction—let alone the relief—of transforming yourself into interesting and bizarre objects such as a phonograph record playing music or a butterfly zooming over fields of flowers. You could dance, fly instantly to other planets, or engage with people in a "normal" body. At the very least this could be considered temporary relief from chronic suffering and psychological respite for those with such limitations.

For the aged, many of whom long to be "young again," this can be achieved during lucid dreams. Your mind may not be younger (and you may not even wish for that), but your body in the dream could be of any age you choose. This approach of compensating for and relieving a difficult situation via lucid dreaming would also be of value to those incarcerated in jails and prisons. The freedoms that they are denied in the daytime can be regained at night. One imagines that under these conditions there would be plenty of time to develop a practice like lucid dreaming.

For those who wish to explore this area using a formal approach, LaBerge offers some excellent strategies in the book mentioned above.

PSYCHOLOGICAL AND PHYSICAL HEALING

In the West there are numerous theories about the mind and the psyche and at least as many approaches to healing psychological problems. As we have seen, lucid dreaming and dream yoga provide an optimal means of exploring consciousness not only in terms of the psyche but from a much deeper perspective. The final phase of dream yoga—facing deep fears and letting frightening scenarios play themselves out—is an excellent means of healing the mind.

If you engage seriously with either lucid dreaming or dream yoga over a long period, you are very likely to dredge up deep and perhaps hidden fears—what the psychologist Carl Jung called the "shadow." Or, to put it simply, you will experience your worst nightmare. Whatever you fear the most will very likely show up during a lucid dream. If this is something you would prefer to avoid at all costs, then the practices of lucid dreaming and dream yoga may not be for you. However, from the standpoint of personal transformation—of freeing yourself from fear—such a nightmare may be a blessing in disguise. The gist of the practice is to "allow the worst to happen" rather than fleeing. If you are dreaming lucidly you know that the object generating your fear—say a monster of some sort or some evil character or force—is only a dream. It has no substance. It is nothing more than a harmless, immaterial appearance emerging from your substrate. If necessary, you can awaken yourself and it will vanish. But it may be of great value to face the fearful object calmly, let it do whatever it wants, and watch what transpires. This therapeutic approach is found in Western psychology as well as in the practices of spiritual traditions.

In Jung's view, dream entities such as monsters and demons indicate that the ego is somehow incomplete. What is required in this approach to healing is that the shadow figures be integrated with the rest of the ego. Stephen LaBerge once had repeated lucid dream encounters with a monster—an experience that may illustrate Jung's hypothesis. As Stephen explained it to me, for a long period a frightening monster appeared regularly in his dreams. At first, being a superb lucid dreamer, he would either escape from the monster, transform it, or transform the dream environment. However, the monster kept returning and LaBerge thought a better approach was required—after all, in a dream, who is escaping from whom? And where are you escaping to? It's a shadow dance.

So he decided to face this fearful image. As he faced this terrifying monster, he looked it in the eyes and had a true encounter with someone who was looking back. He saw a sentient being that had joys and sorrows, hopes and fears like himself. He realized, "Here's a being like myself." And he suddenly felt a burst of loving-kindness, compassion, and empathy, rather than terror, for this creature who was appearing. Then this being simply dissolved into Stephen and it never reappeared. Jung might have commented that some part of LaBerge's psyche had become estranged, creating this monster, and that his act of compassion toward this symbol for the alienated element enabled it to be reintegrated into his psyche.

There are no doubt other approaches that can be developed from lucid dreaming and dream yoga that accommodate themselves to the many other theories, styles, and philosophies of psychological therapy where dreams are used as an important avenue for understanding the psyche. Freud was especially keen on understanding the meaning of dreams for application to psychotherapy. In lucid dreaming, the symbols that are so important for dream analysis are fully within one's grasp—one can interact with them, question them, modify them, obtain an intimate understanding of them. So it would appear that dream yoga would add a dynamism to the therapeutic process, much as hypnosis does in some therapies.

Another possible therapeutic use of lucid dreaming would be in dealing with "unfinished business" with people and situations that cannot be approached directly. This could range from feelings of guilt or resentment toward a deceased relative, friend, or loved one to anxiety over a previous relationship where the other person(s) concerned, though still alive, may not desire contact. In either case, one is usually stuck in a psychologically uncomfortable situation with no effective means of closure. However, in lucid dreams you can conjure up the party with whom you wish to communicate in the form of an image identical to the original. You can pose questions, offer forgiveness, express your feelings, say farewell, and so forth. Of course the entire scenario emerges from your substrate. You are not speaking to the real person. But if you have no other means of, for instance, unburdening yourself of feelings of guilt, the realism of lucid dreaming could be cathartic.

As for using dreams to heal physical problems, there is plenty of anecdotal evidence, and some scientific proof, that healing the mind can positively affect the body. That potential is also suggested in the manipulation of pranic energy in advanced stages of yoga and dream yoga. Stephen LaBerge has posed the following question for future lucid dream research: "If we heal the dream body, to what extent do we heal the physical body?" Medical science, still reluctant to investigate nonmaterial aspects of health and healing, would be wise to investigate this question, given that psychological and spiritual approaches to healing have proven effective over the course of history in a variety of cultural settings, including the modern West. Until then, lucid dreamers may comprise part of a vanguard that will usher in entirely new therapies for some of the diseases medical science and psychiatry have found intractable.

Performance Training and Creativity

Due to the vividness of its imagery and the degree of creative control possible over the environment, the laboratory of lucid dreaming is an ideal location to improve performance and creativity in virtually any realm of human endeavor. Throughout history, many creative works of art and scientific discoveries have been credited to dream revelations. In the realm of athletic performance, Jack Nicklaus, who still holds the record for winning major PGA tournaments, famously improved his golf game through discoveries made in a single lucid dream.

Peak performance training techniques use a combination of affirmations ("I will succeed!") with visualizations to prepare oneself for optimum execution—whether it be a tennis serve, brain surgery, or a violin concerto. Where can affirmation and visualization be more effectively rehearsed than in a lucid dream? In normal visualization techniques, one sits quietly and imagines one is performing a physical movement. Even though one is not moving, a neural connection is made that can enhance an actual performance. As an example, the famed pianist Arthur Rubinstein was known for his ability to mentally practice a piece he had never performed—imagining the fingering while reading the score—and then perform it without any further rehearsal.[1] Research shows that the dream environment is even more effective for establishing neural connections in the absence of actual movements. If you are a pianist, you could have your piano, the auditorium, and even an audience to applaud your lucidly dreamed performance.

If you are uncomfortable performing in public, the lucid dream lab enables you to rehearse that situation until you become accustomed to it. In the case of a business presentation before your boss and senior administrators, you can create an exact replica of the conference room and people it with images that match your audience. You can make them skeptical, see them becoming convinced by your arguments, and finally congratulating you on your presentation. After several such rehearsals, the actual presentation will seem "old hat" to you and you are much more likely to breeze through it having utilized lucid dreaming than you would from other visualization techniques or by attempting the presentation cold.

The topics above are no more than suggestions relating to some of the practical uses to which one can put lucid dreaming and dream yoga. More detailed information can be gleaned from published techniques designed to utilize affirmations, visualization techniques, and the like during waking hours. You need only transfer these exercises to your personal lucid dream laboratory at night. More detailed suggestions and procedures can also be found in the later chapters of Stephen LaBerge's *Exploring the World of Lucid Dreaming*.

9

Individualized Practice and Infrequently Asked Questions

W E ARE EACH UNIQUE. Since the womb, our psyches have developed constantly, their patterns and contents emerging from our experience sui generis. If we accept the idea of a substrate consciousness that has been shaped by our experiences from lifetime to lifetime since beginningless time, our uniqueness is magnified all the more. Therefore, individualized practice for lucid dreaming, dream yoga, or any other approach to spirituality is necessarily nuanced. General guidance is of course helpful, but specific knowledge gained from personal experience and advice from others—especially from an experienced teacher—is beneficial and sometimes crucial.

There are many ways to skin a cat, so throughout *Dreaming Yourself Awake* I have attempted to nuance my presentation such that alternatives are presented whenever possible. I have found that the most useful advice has come from questions and comments given me by my students. Not surprisingly, practitioners of lucid dreaming and dream yoga display a wide variety of backgrounds, philosophical views, and approaches to the topic. Below is a selection that I hope you will find beneficial.

ON DREAM PRACTICES

How to Develop an Overall Practice

Question: Should I plan my practice sessions?

Response: I think it makes good sense to plan. It is important to have balance. Spiritual practice is like eating. A balanced diet is important. Design something that strikes a balance and has a real structure rather than being sporadic about your approach. Bring your intelligence, learning, and experience to the design of your practice. For example: Hatha Yoga can be a meditative practice. You can bring a great deal of mindfulness to it— including mindfulness of breathing. For centering, some type of shamatha practice is good. Then an insight practice such as vipashyana or dream yoga is a mode of inquiry. Finally do something for the heart—the Four Immeasurables, for example. If you do only one of the Four Immeasurables,[1] then do a loving-kindness practice. If you would like a more enriched diet for the heart, then incorporate all four.

It is also very important to do something for your body. That could be a very mindful, vigorous hike to the mountains. Something of your choice for the body, and then the three basic food groups complete the diet. How much of each becomes very individual. Go with the flow and determine what is working for you.

These practices, let's call it Dharma, are all about the cultivation of the causes of genuine happiness (sense of well-being, fulfillment, meaning, joy, satisfaction) that arise independently of external sensory input. These come from the very nature of awareness itself. They carry you through a wide array of circumstances with a sense of well-being.

Spiritual practices, whether Christian, Hindu, Buddhist, Taoist, Sufi, or secular, all seek genuine happiness. As you pragmatically assess your spiritual practice, ask yourself if it is yielding the kind of benefits that you value. Consider the qualities that you would really like to cultivate, behavior you would like to modify, or your general resilience when faced with adversity. Also, what qualities would you like to see attenuated? To what extent is your spiritual practice really nurturing positive qualities? Some people may place a strong emphasis on yoga. For others everything will rotate around the Four Immeasurables or knowledge or insight or service in the world. It is important to assess and modify accordingly.

Advice on Keeping a Dream Journal

Question: I have always had lots of dreams and often write them down. I look for the ones with real power. The mundane dreams I don't bother to write down. Last night I had several dreams, but they were mundane. I thought I would wait until later to write them down, but I forgot them. Do you go to the ones that have the power or the ones that are mundane?

Response: I sympathize and agree with you. The issue of writing down every dream seems monotonous. You would have to have an enormous amount of enthusiasm. However, in the lucid dreaming context, the whole point of writing down the dreams is to enhance dream recall, without which the lucid dreaming practice will have a hard time getting off the ground. So you need a good-sized database.

Even among the mundane dreams you can determine dream signs. This enables you to gather your database in order to recognize your recurrent dream signs. And dream signs might shift, so you need to keep them updated. Also note some of the anomalies and impossibilities that arise. Once you have done this, there is not much reason to keep writing them down.

But it is also important to apply the basic techniques of not moving, of remaining physically still when you awaken, and then reverting your attention back into the dream and seeing if you can gain lucidity. In that case, even if the dream is mundane, it is perfectly good grist for the mill. If you can revert and go back into it with lucidity then you have the possibility of turning it into a very exciting dream. It doesn't have to stay boring since you can direct it as you wish.

"Flat" Lucid Dreams

Question: I have had lucid dreams. I have been aware that the dream is taking place, for instance, when I am flying. But not much comes out of that. The dream just plays itself out and I am just along for the ride. I don't seem to be getting anywhere. Where can I go from here?

Response: Dream yoga takes a much more creative involvement with the contents of the dream and it really tries to deeply fathom dreams in some very interesting ways. So dream yoga is a great platform to make a choice as to whether you would like to venture further along the path of lucid dreaming, perhaps to dream yoga, or leave it right there. There are a lot of very interesting experiments to be run if you wish to venture into a more creative engagement with the dream.

Vividness versus Stability

Question: Can one become so seduced by the vivid aspect of meditation and dream practices such that stability never establishes itself?

Response: A lot of practitioners from different traditions get a taste of the vividness, which is experienced like a "high." And from my generation many people have meditated, and to let the cat out of the bag, a lot of them before they meditated took drugs. They took LSD, mescaline, mushrooms, and so forth. So before they ever meditated they knew something about lucidity in terms of brilliance and vividness—that's where the word "psychedelic" comes from. And then they start tiptoeing into meditation and they have some experiences where there is a high degree of intensity. It's a high—just blazingly present and luminously clear—and they say, "That's for me! This is like drugs without any of the side effects and without doing anything illegal. Give me the high."

And it is very easy when people have had a taste of that to tell themselves they want to have that experience all the time. So they may go exclusively for vividness and say, "Never mind that stability stuff, it's boring. And relaxation, that's for people on vacation." So relaxation is swept away—"Who needs that? And stability, that's just calm, that's just boring." So they go right for vividness. That happens a lot. As a result they become high-strung, they become "wired." They become emotionally very vulnerable, very unstable, and then the high doesn't last. They come out into the world and their practice completely collapses. They are oversensitive to the noise, clutter, and utter rambunctiousness of the everyday world and can't handle it.

Subtle Cues in Realistic Dreams

Question: When dreams are very realistic I have a lot of difficulty becoming lucid. One was a scene from work that happened a number of years ago. In it I met my wife in a library, which is unusual, but only subtly so.

Response: In that regard if you can find *recurrent* dream signs, that could be a cue or an anomaly—such as seeing your wife in a library repeatedly. You had a mild anomaly. Recognition of subtle anomalies is a skill to be developed. Prospective memory especially needs to be honed, and then bring in a critical reflective attitude, asking, "How odd is that?" That can be the catalyst. Develop the habit of looking for anything and everything that is outside the norm.

Reviving a Dream if Your Dream Persona Is Disembodied

Question: In some of my dreams I am disembodied—I have no dream body in the dream. I am just a presence witnessing the dream lucidly. But when the dream starts to fade, I have no body to rub down or to spin to revivify the dream. What can I do to keep the dream going?

Response: You can then jazz it up by anticipating or projecting. Let's imagine you are seeing a country road. You can say to yourself, "I'll bet my friend is just about to come over the horizon driving his cool Maserati." So anticipate like that. This is one of the great come-ons in a dream: anticipation, expectation. These have an enormous influence on dreams. All you have to do is believe or expect or anticipate or even fear that something is going to happen and lo and behold there it is. It's just that simple. And in that way the dream continues.

Semilucid Transformation

Question: A few years ago I had a dream where I was walking along the street, approaching someone, and I had an uncomfortable encounter. In my dream I "backed up the tape" fifty feet and played it back with the encounter edited out. I have never chosen to do this again. Does this have any specific meaning?

Response: That sort of activity occurs right in the middle of the second phase of the dream yoga of transformation. This reminds me of a dream someone shared with me. She was on a skyscraper that was under construction, eighty floors up. While up there she noticed that the actor Mel Gibson was with her. She was talking with Mel Gibson, who suddenly slipped and fell. She said, "No you don't!" Then she edited and replayed the dream so that he didn't fall and plunge to his death. He miraculously rescued himself.

   This is one of those "quasi" areas. Was she lucid? Not necessarily completely, but she was lucid enough that she could intervene and she accomplished what she intended—hanging out with Mel Gibson! So it's within the gray area of lucidity.

Lucid Dreaming and Purification

Question: Can one do purification practices in lucid dream?
Response: Definitely yes.

THE NATURE OF DREAMS

The Variables—Intensty and Lucidity

Question: What is the relationship between the intensity of a dream and the lucidity of a dream?

Response: By intensity we mean the acuity of the dream—the high resolution, the brilliance, the clarity, the vividness of it. The relationship between intensity and lucidity is not one-to-one. You can be lucid in a dream that is rather vague. So these are somewhat independent variables. One may have a very intense dream in which one has no lucidity at all—one is totally caught up in it. And such dreams can be very emotionally charged.

Having said that, in a dream-initiated lucid dream (DILD), lucidity is more likely to be internally catalyzed by an intense dream rather than a rather dull, vague one. That is because if there are anomalies in the dream, and most dreams do have them, then the anomalies will be more vivid, which means they are more likely to catch your attention, perhaps leading to the critical reflective attitude and the observation, "That was so strange!" And that may catalyze lucidity.

So the two are independent, and they are expressing different types of luminosity. When you speak of an intense dream, all you are really speaking about is the sheer vividness of attention displayed quite flamboyantly. It doesn't necessarily mean there is a great vividness of *cognizance*. There is also another kind of clarity, and that is the clarity of *insight*. And that doesn't necessarily go along with some clear, extremely vivid, image. It means, "I totally get it. I really fathom this." It may be something that has no visual image at all, but the clarity of one's insight is razor sharp. That's the vividness, the acuity, the sharpness of knowing. That's related to, but not the same as, simple vividness of attention.

So the optimal situation is to combine those two, where the luminosity or vividness of attention is being displayed quite evidently—so there you get the intense dream—and couple that with the clarity, the vividness, the high acuity of knowing, of cognizance. Then you have a very intense, very lucid dream.

Follow-up question: How do you do that?

Response: Practice shamatha and dream yoga.

Dreaming and Daydreaming

Question: How does daydreaming relate to dreaming?

Response: Daydreaming is a form of unedited imagination. We simply let the attention rove. We may take a special interest in daydreaming a story line, image, memory, or fantasy that we are drawn to, in which case grasping will set in and we try and maintain it, pursue it, and develop it. What makes daydreaming sometimes enjoyable or sometimes painful is that they are all products of the imagination. As the neuroscientist Francisco Varela commented, when we are engaged in acts of imagination, seeing things in our mind's eye, there is a great deal of overlap in terms of brain activity between what we are perceiving in imagination or daydreaming and what we perceive in normal daily activity. Our overall perception of the world is in fact a result of an active imagination with ordinary physical constraints. Dreaming is similar—perception without physical constraints. The three are all bundled together—perception, imagination, and dreaming.

THE SOURCES OF DREAMING

Dream Origins

Question: Dreams don't evolve entirely from the substrate. Where do the contents of dreams come from?

Response: There is some correlation to the sleep cycles, but this is just a generalization. The night can be divided into three sections. It is said that the dreams in the early part of the night (the first one or two cycles) will likely be short and conditioned by and inspired by recent events. There is often a strong correlation with events of the preceding day in the waking state. There is not much of a time buffer between them, only about ninety minutes after you fall asleep. The dream cycle is very short. The origin of this material is the psyche.

In the middle part of the night there is more of a time buffer separating you from the previous day, so you may be tapping into older memories. The origin is still the psyche. If one is going to have meaningful or precognitive dreams or remote viewing dreams (common especially if there is a blood connection with the person seen), the prime time for significant dreams is that of the final dreams at the end of the night. They are tapping more deeply into the substrate. These may be inspired by childhood dreams or even past lifetimes.

If you are tapping deeply into the substrate, you might catalyze some memory in a past life. But this does not explain precognition or remote viewing. The substrate is in conventional reality; it is local, personal, and accumulates memories. It is on a conventional, relative plane. As you are encroaching upon the substrate you are encroaching upon memories. But shafts of light from primordial consciousness may beam through, especially when there is a strong karmic relationship (teacher and student, mother and child, close friendships). It's like a wormhole stemming from primordial consciousness and opening up in your substrate consciousness. It can tap into your network of karma. The emphasis here tends to be on the last two hours of sleep.

Karma as the Basis of Dreams

Question: As causes and conditions present at any given moment contribute to the germination of karmic seeds stored in the substrate, would not each dream be a result of karma arising?

Response: It all depends on how you define karma, but the short answer would be no. When you accumulate karma by means of any voluntary action of body, speech, or mind, then the Buddhist understanding is that karmic seeds or imprints are then implanted and stored in the substrate consciousness. They may remain there for years or even lifetimes until eventually they are catalyzed by some external or internal circumstance that then, metaphorically, germinates and the karma manifests. So one speaks of that as the fruition of karma, and it comes to fruition in various ways.

Dreams are not just the result of karma. For example, you might eat some food that is very difficult to digest just before you go to bed. And then you might have some dreams that are nightmarish that are being strongly influenced by your indigestion. That's not really due to karma but to indigestion. So that's a much more proximate catalyst for arousing bad dreams or restless sleep and so forth.

Or let's imagine you had a very anxious day—maybe someone rear-ended your car and they showed you a false driver's license and false insurance certificate, all leading to a dead end. So if that experience occupies the day, then at night you might have a dream corresponding to something very similar. That's not the fruition of karma. That's just memory carrying over and perhaps taking on a new permutation in the dream—daytime experience influencing nighttime experience.

To the question, "Can karma come to maturation in the

dream state?" The answer is "definitely yes." But many other things manifest in the dream state as well. For those of you who are Buddhists, note that the process of purifying the mind from quite a deep place by way of Vajrasattva meditation, for instance, can actually catalyze karma, which will come to fruition in your dreams. And that's one way of purifying the karma, rather than having it come to full maturation in some waking state. Better to get rid of it in the dream state.

MISCELLANEOUS TOPICS

Influence of Food on Meditation; Doing Back-to-Back Practice Sessions

Question: I've noticed that my meditation focus is not so sharp after eating—it bounces around. Does eating before practice generally cause problems? And what contexts are more conducive to practice?

Response: This depends on how well you digest your food and on whether you've eaten a healthy amount. You might want to let your food settle before you formally meditate. Then a combination that can be very helpful is two back-to-back sessions. They don't need to be short, whatever duration you like. Do the first session in the supine position focusing on full-body awareness and mindfulness of breathing with a primary emphasis on groundedness, the sensation of firmness of the body on the ground and overwhelmingly an emphasis on relaxation to soothe and ground the mind and body. Then after this session, sit up and do the practice of awareness of awareness. The two together—grounding and resting in the space of awareness—can be very effective.

Ethics in Lucid Dreams

Question: Can ethics be of any importance in lucid dreams? After all, if you commit some negative act there, it's all a dream. There is really no one who is harmed.

Response: Motivation is crucial and profound. Within the context of the dream, recognize that even though there is no one who will be benefited or harmed by your acts (unlike in the waking state), nevertheless the fact that you engaged in a negative attitude has ethical import or gravity. Some people who have no moral context think they can do whatever they wish. You can do what you wish, but the impact on your mind and the ethical implications of this are important.

The Source of Teachings Received in Lucid Dreams

Question: What attitude should I take regarding teachings and advice I receive from people I meet in lucid dreams? Are these coming from wisdom?

Response: It could be delusional, terrible advice—or sublime advice. The Buddha encouraged his followers not to accept his words simply on the basis of his authority. By means of reason and experience, carefully check the validity of teachings, whether during the waking state or while dreaming. Accept them if they strike you as being sound.

At the same time go back to the archetypal issues. Say there is someone you deeply revere, for example, Saint Francis of Assisi. When you seek out Saint Francis in your dream, you may be tapping into the deepest reservoirs of your own wisdom. If you should meet the Buddha and he gives you sublime teachings, imagine they really do work. The question can be raised here: What is the source of the advice you are receiving? It could be coming from primordial consciousness manifesting by way of your lama. If so, it's not the lama's primordial consciousness versus yours. At that level they are undifferentiated.

10

Dreaming Yourself Awake

A Wider Perspective

IN ONE OF MY FIRST LUCID DREAMS, I was riding in a car on a desert road and noticed the sun rising to my left, and a little while later I saw it setting in the same direction. How odd was that? Too odd! And that was what alerted me to the fact that I had to be dreaming. I knew precisely the moment I became lucid, but when did the dream start? Evidently, when that dream first began, I wasn't aware that I was dreaming, so later on I had no recollection of *what* I wasn't aware of earlier, namely the beginning of the dream. The dream began in unawareness (*avidya*), or ignorance, and since I wasn't aware of the nature of the reality I was experiencing, I came to regard it simply as "real," without drawing any distinction between waking reality and dreaming reality. So unawareness led to delusion.

THE PROCESS OF DELUSION

According to Buddhist philosophy, something is said to be existent if it is knowable and nonexistent if it is unknowable. We may not be aware of it yet. We may never be aware of it. But if it is knowable by anyone, it is said to exist. Or to turn this on its head: if something exists, it must be knowable by someone. In a nonlucid dream, there is no awareness of the beginning of the dream as a dream. At the beginning was unawareness, which gave way to the delusion of misapprehending the dream for something it isn't—for something that is real. If one had recognized the dream as a dream from the start, one would have been lucid right from its beginning. But since the dream began nonlucidly, the first moment of the dream—emerging from unawareness—is unknowable by the dreamer. And since it is unknowable in principle from within that context, the beginning of the dream doesn't exist for the dreamer. The nonlucid dream is rooted in delusion, and that traces back to unawareness, the beginning of which is unknowable. Once one has become lucid, one may remember earlier phases of the dream, but that doesn't mean one has traced it back to its very beginning.

The same holds true for an absentminded wandering thought. While meditating, when we suddenly notice that our attention has been carried away by some distracting thought, we become "lucid" with respect to that thought. We recognize this mental event as a mental event and don't mistake it for the referent of the thought in the outer world. But when we try to trace that thought back to its origin, we fail. This chain of thought began in unawareness, which is why we were absentminded. If we had recognized the thought as a thought from its inception, we would have been "lucid" from the very beginning of that thought. But since there was no awareness of the thought as a thought when it first arose, there is no possibility of later remembering what we never knew in the first place. From within the context of that string of absentminded thoughts, its beginning is unknowable and therefore doesn't exist for that thinker even after one has become lucid with respect to one's thoughts by recognizing them for what they are.

Each time we are "born" into a sequence of absentminded thoughts, we enter a microcosm of samsara. This chain of thoughts arose from unawareness, and as soon as we become caught up in such obsessive, compulsive thinking, we are prone to mistake our thoughts for a reality that is independent of our minds. Ignorance leads to delusion, and that easily leads to all other mental afflictions, including craving and hostility. And from the perspective of that cycle of obsessive conceptualization, there is no identifiable beginning. In the same way, whenever we are "born" into a nonlucid dream, we enter a microcosm of samsara, originating in unawareness, unfolding in delusion, and proliferating in habitual patterns of craving and aversion.

According to the Buddha's teachings, samsara has no identifiable beginning. It is said to be beginningless, but does this literally mean that each of us has had an infinite number of previous lives? If so, might we have only an infinitesimal chance of achieving liberation this time around or in any future life? That's a dismal outlook, so maybe there is an alternative to an overly literal interpretation of the "beginningless" nature of samsara. Perhaps samsara is beginningless only in the sense that its beginning is *unknowable,* as is the number of our past lives.

According to the classic teachings on the twelve links of dependent origination,[1] based on the Buddha's contemplative discoveries during the night of his enlightenment, the cycle of rebirth emerges from ignorance of central facets of reality, such as the Four Noble Truths. Out of this unawareness arise mental formations, energetic impulses that structure our being and form the basis of our character. In dependence upon those mental formations arises a partially structured dimension of consciousness that shapes the energetic activity of mental formations into more crystallized, reified forms. Once that stage of consciousness has arisen, "name and form" appear, when experience becomes bifurcated into subjectively experienced mental functions (*nama*) that are involved in naming things and objectively experienced appearances (*rupa*) that are classified and named. In this way the unity of the flow of experience subjectively arises as the identification of appearances and things (*nama*) and objectively arises as the appearances and entities that are identified. Mental cognition (*manas*) is the mental process of conceptualization that integrates and makes meaning out of the different percepts brought in through the six senses.[2] According to this view, the mind and matter are not two separate, independent entities that somehow come together and interact with each other. Rather, they are categories conceived from a flow of experience that is more fundamental than either of these derivative classes of phenomena. The mind-body problem is one that originates from the conceptual mind, so the mind that reifies this duality is incapable of solving the problem it created.

DUALISM: THE EMERGENCE OF SUBJECT AND OBJECT

A similar account of the origins of samsara is presented in the Dzogchen tradition of Buddhism. Each cycle of samsara begins in unawareness of the ground of being, known as the absolute space of phenomena (*dharamdhatu*), which is indivisible from primordial consciousness (*jñana*). This state of unawareness corresponds to the experience of the substrate (*alaya*), a blank, unthinking void, immaterial like space and empty of appearances. From this state emerge movements of karmic energies that begin to crystallize one's experience, and in dependence upon their movements arises the substrate consciousness (*alayavijñana*), a radiant, clear dimension of consciousness that is the basis of the emergence of appearances. Everything that appears consists of displays of the luminosity of the substrate consciousness, and while it can give rise to all kinds of appearances, it does not enter into any object. From the substrate consciousness emerges afflictive cognition (*klishtamanas*) that congeals the sense of "I am" over here, in opposition to the space of the substrate "over there." Following that arises mental cognition (*manas*), which differentiates between objective appearances emerging in the immaterial space of the substrate

and subjective mental processes arising from the substrate consciousness.[3]

The conceptual categories of mind and matter, embedded in
the large framework of the constructs of subject and object,
emerge out of a flow of experience that precedes and is more
primal than these concepts. Both classical Buddhism as recorded in the Pali Canon[4] and the Dzogchen tradition reject
monistic materialism (the view that everything boils down to
space, time, matter, and energy and their derivative or emergent
properties) and substance dualism (the theory that the world is
fundamentally composed of two kinds of real, inherently different entities: mind and matter). The categories of mind and matter are constructs conceived out of the flow of experience, which
exists prior to the differentiation of "outer" and "inner," "subject" and "object."

The pioneering American psychologist William James proposed a similar theory that might have revolutionized the mind
sciences if they hadn't subsequently been dominated by the
metaphysical assumptions of materialism. He rejected that either mind or matter is a primal stuff out of which subjective and
objective phenomena emerge and proposed instead that these
constructs are formulated out of a flow of "pure experience,"
which has the potential to manifest as mind and matter.[5] While
the nature of such pure experience may be explored by way
of introspection and various contemplative practices, it is experimentally inaccessible to the materialistic methods of modern psychology and neuroscience. So this hypothesis has not
been pursued by the scientific community. Instead, cognitive
scientists rely on their objective systems of inquiry, including
questionnaires, behavioral studies, and the study of neurophysi-
ological processes. Unless scientists interview someone with direct knowledge of pure experience, they will not gain even
indirect knowledge of this dimension of consciousness and are
therefore likely to remain trapped in their unquestioned and

therefore uncorroborated materialistic assumptions about the origins and nature of consciousness.

The belief that all subjective experience must arise from matter stems from the scientific view of the history of the universe. According to this narrative, the cosmos originated from the Big Bang, out of which emerged space-time and mass-energy, which began to form into galaxies around four hundred million years after the big bang. Roughly five billion years ago, our planet was formed, and two or three billion years later the first life forms emerged and life has evolved through natural selection and genetic mutation ever since. If we believe this to be the one true history of the universe, then life must have evolved from non-living matter, and consciousness must have emerged from organic physical processes. However, there are no scientifically testable hypotheses about the conditions that led to the big bang, to the initial emergence of life on our planet, to the emergence of consciousness in the first sentient organisms, or to the emergence of consciousness in a human fetus. All the scientists have come up with are materialist speculations, none of which have been corroborated. This ignorance of origins may imply that not all the causes and conditions that led to the formation of the physical universe, life, and consciousness are physical. Indeed, it seems a bit presumptuous to assume that the entire universe consists only of the kinds of phenomena that scientists are capable of measuring, namely, objective, physical, quantifiable ones.

MIND AND MATTER IN MODERN PHYSICS

While the standard view of the origin and evolution of the cosmos, based on the mechanistic, materialist assumptions of nineteenth-century physics, dominates scientific thinking to this day, it has been challenged by some of the most brilliant theoretical physicists of recent times. Stephen Hawking, for instance, has proposed that there is no absolutely objective history of the universe as it exists independently of all systems of measurement and conceptual modes of inquiry. Indeed, many quantum physicists adhere to the maxim *do not attribute existence to that which is unknowable in principle.* The universe as it exists independently of all systems of measurement is a prime case of something that is unknowable in principle. So we have no reasonable grounds for asserting its existence, and even if we do, we are affirming the existence of something about which we know nothing except that it must exist—and that's a marginal kind of knowledge at best.

In quantum physics it is widely accepted that prior to making a measurement, the system to be measured exists in a state of quantum superposition, mathematically described as a probability wave. It is important to recognize that the probability wave is not something objectively out there, waiting to "collapse" when a measurement is made. Rather, it is a mathematical description that pertains to the probabilistic results of making a measurement. Before the measurement takes place, there are no discrete elementary particles with objectively real locations or velocities in the system to be measured, and nothing can be said about what is really there objectively. Actualization of these particles and their properties occurs only with the act of measurement.

Applying the principles of quantum physics to the universe at large, Hawking suggests that before making measurements, every possible version of a single universe exists simultaneously in a state of quantum superposition. When scientists choose to make a measurement, they select from this range of possibilities a subset of histories that share the specific features measured. This implies that the universe did not evolve in an absolutely unique and real way prior to the measurements we make in the present. Scientists decide what measurements to make, and the information that is provided by those measurements provides the basis for the descriptions they formulate about the past. The history of the universe as they conceive of it exists relative to the measurements they have conducted, but not independently of those measurements. Ask a different set of questions, resulting in a different set of measurements, and another history arises relative to the information gleaned from those measurements. In other words, scientists choose a history of the universe based on the types of measurements they conduct.[6] In his latest book, *A Grand Design*, coauthored with Leonard Mlodinow, Hawking suggests that physicists may never find a theory of everything but must rather be satisfied with a "family of interconnected theories," each one bearing truths relative to the kinds of measurements on which they are based.

John Wheeler, another of the preeminent theoretical physicists of the late twentieth century, proposed a similar theory in which he described a "strange loop," in which physics gives rise to observers and observers give rise to at least part of physics.[7] According to the standard history of the universe outlined above, the physical world gave rise to scientific observers, who have made measurements of material processes from which they have acquired information about the natural world. This implies the classical sequence of matter → information → observers. From the perspective of quantum physics, however, the *information* derived from measurements—and not matter—is fundamental. All that we fundamentally know about nature consists of such information, and out of that information scientists have formulated the concepts of space, time, mass, and energy. It takes an observer for information to emerge from a measurement, and the conceptual category of *matter* emerges from that information. So this implies a reversed sequence from that of classical physics, namely: observers → information → matter. Rather than the universe being a mindless machine fundamentally composed of matter and energy, Wheeler describes it as an information-processing system in which observer-participants play a fundamental role in the emergence of the natural world. But to understand this role requires an understanding of consciousness, for there are no unconscious observers.

There Is No Universe without Consciousness

There is no such thing as information without the presence of a conscious agent who is informed and without the presence of something about which that agent is informed. Likewise, there is no informed subject without the presence of information, and there is nothing about which one is informed if there is not the act of being informed and someone who is informed. The three—the informed subject, the imparting of information, and the object about which one is informed—are all mutually interdependent. So, from one perspective it is still true that matter gives rise to information, which gives rise to observers; and from another perspective, it is the observer who gives rise to information, from which matter is conceived. That, in short, is Wheeler's "strange loop," in which we humans are observer-participants who co-create the world of our experience, while uncritically assuming that it already exists out there, independent of our participation. Our waking reality is therefore like a nonlucid dream, from which we awake only when we recognize the extent of our participation in the creation of the world we experience.

Over the past four hundred years since the rise of modern science, the first great scientific revolution took place in the physical sciences in the seventeenth century. When Darwin initiated the second great scientific revolution in the nineteenth century, he could only conclude that life originated from and evolved due to physical processes, for those were the only ones scientists knew anything about. And when the mind sciences began to develop in the late nineteenth century, cognitive scientists had no alternative but to assume that consciousness and all subjective experiences arose from biological processes, for scientists at that time knew only about inorganic and organic physical processes. The history of science moves from advances in physics to biology to psychology, and this sequence is exactly replicated on a cosmic scale in scientists' depiction of the history of the universe:

first there were inorganic physical processes, then organic ones, then the emergence of consciousness. In other words, the scientific history of the universe is a macrocosmic projection of the history of science over the past four hundred years. That history is based on measurements made first by physicists, then by biologists, and finally by psychologists, and it is true only relative to those measurements but not independently of them.

Standard textbook histories of the cosmos commonly make no reference to consciousness at all. They simply focus on the evolution of the physical universe from the time of the big bang until the present, and if the emergence of consciousness is even mentioned, it is simply regarded as a by-product of complex configurations of matter. There is no explanation of how matter gives rise to consciousness, nor is there any evidence that this theory is even true. It is simply an unavoidable implication of a history of the universe that is based purely on physical measurements. Ask a physical question, and you'll get a physical answer. Scientists have excelled at measuring objective, physical, quantitative phenomena, so they have collectively come to the conclusion that the universe must consist solely of objective, physical, quantitative phenomena and their derivative, or emergent, properties. That is the history of the universe they have chosen, but it is not the only rational or empirical choice.

Regarding the origins of human consciousness, William James proposed three theories: (1) the brain produces thoughts, as an electric circuit produces light; (2) the brain enables, or permits, mental events, as the trigger of a crossbow releases an arrow by removing the obstacle that holds the string; and (3) the brain transmits thoughts, as a prism transmits light, refracting it into a spectrum of colors.[8] He added that the known correlations between neural activity and subjective experience were compatible with all three of those hypotheses, and this remains true to this day. But neuroscientists have no way of measuring mental events that may be only "enabled" or "transmitted" by the brain. They can measure only physical processes in the brain, so it is easiest for them to embrace the first of the above theories, namely, that the brain produces all subjective experiences. But since all known mind-brain correlations are compatible with all three hypotheses, it follows that there is no empirical evidence that the first hypothesis is uniquely true.

James believed that when brain function ceases at death, the individual stream of consciousness that it configured vanishes, but a more fundamental dimension of consciousness from which it emerged would continue.[9] Many scientists might argue that there is no evidence to support this hypothesis, but since all the evidence, or information, neuroscientists have about consciousness is based on brain activity, this reasoning is completely circular. If you ask only physical questions and make physical measurements pertaining to consciousness, you will get only physical answers, and the conclusion that consciousness is totally dependent on brain function is inevitable. In other words, one's starting assumption and all one's subsequent measurements lead to only one possible conclusion, which is identical to one's initial assumption.

From the perspective of twentieth-century physics, the physical universe described by Newton was an imaginary one, for it assumed that space, time, mass, and energy are absolutes, retaining the same characteristics regardless of inertial frames of reference. Such a universe doesn't exist, but that is not apparent as long as one focuses entirely on relatively large objects traveling at nonrelativistic velocities. Similarly, the universe described by modern science is an imaginary one, for it assumes that consciousness accidentally arose from complex interactions of organic processes, and that it plays no significant role in the natural world. Such a universe doesn't exist, but that is not apparent as long as one focuses entirely on physical processes and their interactions with coarse levels of consciousness.

When the principles of quantum physics are applied to the entire universe, as presented in quantum cosmology, the role of the observer-participant is fundamental. And there is no observer-participant apart from consciousness. So this implies that consciousness is as fundamental to the cosmos as space-time and mass-energy, as suggested by the Stanford physicist Andrei Linde,[10] and contrary to the speculative notion that it magically emerges from the chemicals and electricity in the brain, like a genie popping out of a bottle.

Physicists, however, have no training to help them explore the nature or potentials of consciousness and its role in the world of nature. In the meantime, cognitive scientists generally have little if any training in cutting-edge, contemporary physics, so they rely on the outdated metaphysical assumptions of nineteenth-century classical physics. When even some of the finest minds in physics do address the issue of consciousness, they unfortunately rely on the materialistic assumptions of cognitive scientists, which are out of synch with contemporary physics. In a recent interview, Hawking, for instance, simply echoed one of the uncorroborated assumptions of modern neuroscience when he replied to the question of what he believes happens to consciousness after death: "I think the brain is essentially a computer and consciousness is like a computer program. It will cease to run when the computer is turned off."[11] Once again, without any corroborating evidence it is assumed—with no cogent explanation of how the chemicals and electricity in the brain produce or transform into subjective experience—that consciousness is nothing more than a product of brain circuitry. Here physics comes to an impasse, and the twentieth-century revolution in physics is stalled due to an inadequate understanding of the nature of consciousness and its role in the universe.

THE CONTINUITY OF CONSCIOUSNESS

The origin of consciousness is an absentminded sequence of wandering thoughts shrouded in unawareness, as is the origin of consciousness in a nonlucid dream. According to Vajrayana

Buddhism, the origin of ordinary human consciousness is also shrouded in unawareness. Just as primordial consciousness manifests as the clear light of death immediately during the dying process, so does it manifest as the clear light of birth at the time of conception. But for ordinary beings, this pristine awareness flashes by unrecognized, and it is immediately eclipsed by the unconscious emergence of the substrate. Karmic energies then catalyze this immaterial vacuity, out of which the substrate consciousness emerges, and during the formation of the fetus, the human mind forms in dependence upon the developing nervous system.

The scientific search for the neural correlates of consciousness—which has met with little success—is based on the uncorroborated assumption that consciousness emerges from complex interactions of neuronal activity. The hypothetical neural correlates of consciousness are presumed to constitute the minimal degree of such activity needed to generate consciousness. But contrary to the materialistic assumption, if consciousness is simply configured by brain activity, rather than being produced by it, this scientific quest is in vain, for it is based on a false assumption. When scientists speculate about the origins of consciousness on our planet, once again they present only uncorroborated assumptions but not scientifically testable hypotheses. The necessary and sufficient causes and conditions for the emergence of consciousness are simply unknown by the scientific community, so it is equally ignorant about what happens to consciousness at death. Lacking any means to test any nonphysical hypotheses about the nature and origins of consciousness, scientists rely solely on their physical measures, which inevitably lead to physicalist theories of consciousness.

By implementing such meditative practices as shamatha, vipashyana, and Dzogchen, Buddhist contemplatives are able to test their hypotheses experientially, and this has been done repeatedly over hundreds of years in multiple societies. In light of the rich history of the rational and experiential investigation of consciousness in various Buddhist traditions, it is puzzling that so many modern, contemporary teachers of Buddhism are so nonchalant about what happens at death. Placing little if any credence in the centuries of contemplative discoveries by earlier generations of Buddhist contemplatives, tracing back to the Buddha's own discoveries on the night of his enlightenment, they regard the issues of rebirth and karma as irrelevant to spiritual practice. Their rationale seems to be that it is sufficient simply to be present in the here and now and to lead a good life, and let the future take care of itself. But many of these same people are careful to purchase health insurance and save up pensions for their old age, even though they may not become seriously ill or live long enough to benefit from their savings. Such people are taking their future seriously only within the context of this life but completely disregard the possibility that their future may extend far beyond this lifetime.

Traditionally, the idea of being a Buddhist corresponds to taking refuge in the Buddha, Dharma, and Sangha, which implies a deep sense of trust and commitment to the enlightenment of the Buddha, his teachings, and in his spiritually realized followers, as described in the most authoritative texts available. Such trust and commitment to these "Three Jewels" appear to be lacking in those who dismiss the Buddha's insights and teachings on the continuity of consciousness from one birth to the next. Without considering the consequences of one's actions in future lives, the entire focus of one's attention will be on this life alone. Only this life is deemed real and worthy of consideration. For most of us, in this lifetime our chances of achieving an arhat's liberation from the cycle of birth and death are slim, for we are simply not devoting sufficient time and energy to that pursuit. If all that matters to us is our well-being in this lifetime, then the aspiration for liberation will not arise. The entire gist of the Four Noble Truths is thereby undermined. Moreover, the likelihood of our achieving the enlightenment of a buddha is even slimmer, so if we give no thought to future lives, then the bodhisattva's aspiration to achieve enlightenment for the sake of all sentient beings will also not arise. The root of the bodhisattva way of life is thereby severed.

Some teachers of Buddhism go so far as to deny that the Buddha even claimed to have direct insight into the reality of rebirth and karma. We are all perfectly free to believe whatever we like, and the Buddha himself encouraged his followers to put all his teachings to the test of reason and experience. But on the basis of unprofessional scholarship driven by personal biases, some Buddhist revisionists re-create the Buddha according to their own ideas and personal experience and then "take refuge" in their own fantasies about who the Buddha *really* was and what he *really* taught. On the one hand, this misrepresentation of the Buddha's life and teachings may seem harmless—people have the freedom of speech to teach and write whatever they like. But, on the other hand, if it is fraudulent for street peddlers to sell cheap Rolex knockoffs as the real thing, it is just as fraudulent for teachers to peddle their own speculations as authentic teachings of the Buddha.

This does not mean that one must accept Buddhist theories about consciousness before one can venture into Buddhist practice. The Buddha never demanded that his followers believe anything he said. All that is traditionally required of students of Buddhism is to be open-minded, perceptive, and devoted to seeking liberation through the cultivation of insight and understanding.[12] Through such practices as shamatha, vipashyana, and Dzogchen, those with strong determination, who are willing to devote their lives to such inquiry, may put the Buddhist hypotheses to the test of experience and reason. Those who lack such dedication may simply remain agnostic (unknowing), but they should bear in mind that in the Buddhist view, unknowing, or ignorance, is the root of samsara, not the path to liberation. Others may develop sufficient confidence in the integrity of Buddhist contemplatives over the centuries that they come to trust their insights. In the modern world, such trust is commonly placed in the scientific community, and often with good reason. But when it comes to consciousness, metaphysical assumptions are commonly substituted for empirically validated hypotheses, and this tendency has caused endless confusion.

The origins of deluded consciousness are shrouded in unawareness, which leads to the Buddhist conclusion that samsara has no beginning. But is there any end of delusion? Some Buddhists, having practiced for decades without finding complete freedom from their mental afflictions, have dismissed as "misleading" all traditional claims attributed to the Buddha and many later adepts that complete and irreversible freedom is possible. Rather than reassessing their own practice to see what may be deficient, they reinterpret the Buddha's teachings so that it accords more with the assumptions of modern psychoanalysis. Other Buddhist teachers, strictly adhering to tradition and what they deem to be "pure Dharma," so emphasize the importance of future lives that they hardly seem to notice whether their students are truly benefiting from their practice in this life. This attitude may stem from the belief that we are now living in such degenerate times that no one can realistically strive for liberation or enlightenment in this lifetime. Whether that assumption is true or not remains to be seen, but it will be those who are fully committed to reaching the Buddhist path and following it to its culmination who find out for themselves whether such freedom is possible in this lifetime.

As William James declared, for the class of truths that depend on personal preference, trust, or loyalty for actualization, "faith is not only licit and pertinent, but essential and indispensable. [Such] truths cannot become true till our faith has made them so."[13] Is it possible to awaken from this dream of samsara by experientially knowing the nature of consciousness and its role in the universe? Only if we take this possibility as our working hypothesis and apply ourselves wholeheartedly to testing it in the most rigorous ways we can.

Notes

Introduction

1. Stephen LaBerge, "Lucid Dreaming: Psychophysiological Studies of Consciousness during REM Sleep," in *Sleep and Cognition,* ed. R. R. Bootzen, J. F. Kihlstrom, and D. L. Schacter (Washington, D.C.: American Psychological Association, 1990), 109–26.

Chapter 1. Meditative Quiescence: Laying the Groundwork for Lucidity

1. Such a high degree of concentration is called "one-pointedness" (Sanskrit: *ekāgratā*).
2. If you don't believe that grogginess and forgetfulness dominate sleep and dreams, spend a couple of days examining and comparing the sharpness of your attention during the day versus the night and early morning.
3. These side effects include increased physical energy, mental and physical bliss, and greatly heightened mental stability and vividness.
4. B. Alan Wallace, *The Attention Revolution* (Somerville, Mass.: Wisdom Publications, 2006).
5. Enter this position by lying on your back with your spine in a straight line that begins at your head and continues to your heels, which are together with the feet relaxed to

each side. Your arms are straight and at a slight angle away from the body with the palms turned upward.

6. Shantideva, *A Guide to the Bodhisattva Way of Life*, trans. Vesna A. Wallace and B. Alan Wallace (Ithaca, N.Y.: Snow Lion Publications, 1997), V: 108.

CHAPTER 2. THE THEORY OF LUCID DREAMING

1. There were earlier pioneers, including the Marquis d'Hervey de Saint Denys in the nineteenth century. In 1867 he anonymously published a book entitled *Les rêves et les moyens de les diriger; observations pratiques* (*Dreams and the Ways to Direct Them: Practical Observations*).

2. In one Buddhist critique of Indian philosophies, the single example resembling modern scientific materialism (that of the Indian thinker Cārvāka, seventh century B.C.E.) was rejected almost out of hand. P. T. Raju, *Structural Depths of Indian Thought* (Albany, N.Y.: SUNY Press, 1985), ch. 3.

3. Compiled in the eleventh century C.E. by the Indian Buddhist monk Naropa, these six are the advanced practices of *tummo* (inner heat), the yoga of illusory body, the yoga of clear light, dream yoga, the yoga of the intermediary state (of the after-death *bardo*), and the yoga of transference of consciousness (*phowa*). See Tsong-Kha-Pa, *The Six Yogas of Naropa: Tsongkhapa's Commentary Entitled "A Book of Three Inspirations: A Treatise on the Stages of Training in the Profound Path of Naro's Six Dharmas," Commonly Referred to as "The Three Inspirations"*; trans. Glenn H. Mullin (Ithaca N.Y.: Snow Lion Publications, 2005)

4. Padmasambhava, *Natural Liberation: Padmasambhava's Teachings on the Six Bardos,* commentary by Gyatrul Rinpoche, trans. B. Alan Wallace (Boston: Wisdom Publications, 2008).

5. National Sleep Foundation web site (www.sleepfoundation .org), "How Sleep Works" (accessed May 2010).

6. Stephen LaBerge, *Lucid Dreaming: The Power of Being Awake & Aware in Your Dreams* (New York: Ballantine Books, 1985), 14.

Chapter 3. The Practice of Lucid Dreaming

1. National Sleep Foundation.
2. The term "space of the mind" applies to the domain of mental, as opposed to sensory, experience. It is especially evident during the intervals between thoughts, but it is always present as the space from which thoughts emerge, in which they are present, and into which they finally dissolve.

Chapter 4. Proficiency in Lucid Dreaming

1. The intermediate state between one life and the next.

Chapter 5. The Universe of Dream Yoga

1. Cf. B. Alan Wallace, *The Taboo of Subjectivity: Toward a New Science of Consciousness* (New York: Oxford University Press, 2000).
2. D. Shastri, *Tattvasaṃgraha* (Varanasi: Bauddhabharati, 1968), 3587.
3. *The American Heritage Medical Dictionary Online,* s.v. "psyche," http://medical-dictionary.thefreedictionary.com (accessed May 2011).
4. In Buddhism, *primordial consciousness* has numerous synonyms, including *dharmakaya*, pristine awareness, buddha-nature, *rigpa*, and absolute bodhichitta.
5. According to the Dzogchen school of thought, the substrate (Skt. *ayala*) is a luminous vacuity, a blank, unthinking void, immaterial like space, in which self, others, and objects disappear. The substrate is the space of the mind that appears to the substrate consciousness, a radiant, clear dimension of consciousness that is the basis of the emergence of appearances. This, the ground of the ordinary mind, from which springs all ordinary mental

activity, flows from lifetime to lifetime. Since the distinction between the two is subtle, the term "substrate consciousness" will be used for the most part in this text.

6. "[A] second psychic system of a collective, universal, and impersonal nature which is identical in all individuals. This collective unconscious does not develop individually but is inherited. It consists of pre-existent forms, the archetypes, which can only become conscious secondarily and which give definite form to certain psychic contents." C. G. Jung, *The Archetypes and the Collective Unconscious* (London: Routledge, 1996).

7. Generally speaking, this term refers to unenlightened beings possessing minds and who therefore are capable of thinking, feeling, and perceiving.

8. Called the Great Vehicle, this school of Buddhism arose in India in the first century C.E., emphasizing the intention to liberate all beings. Its most important exemplars aside from Tibetan Buddhism are the Chinese Ch'an school, various Pure Land schools, and Zen.

9. A text by Langri Tangpa. See "Commentary on 'The Eight Verses on the Training of the Mind' and Commentary on 'The Song of the Four Mindfulnesses,'" in H. H. the XIV Dalai Lama, *Four Essential Buddhist Commentaries* (Dharamsala: Library of Tibetan Works & Archives, 1982).

CHAPTER 6. THE DAYTIME PRACTICES OF DREAM YOGA

1. Note that Padmasambhava takes a particular Buddhist view related to the Dzogchen and Madhyamaka schools, and although there are other Buddhist philosophies, it is this one that we are emphasizing here.

2. Excerpted from a dream yoga retreat led by Chagdud Rinpoche in 1996 in Monterey Park, California.

3. Antonio Damasio, *The Feeling of What Happens: Body and Emotion in the Making of Consciousness* (New York: Harcourt, 1999), 321.

4. For vivid accounts of such demonstrations that seem to break the laws of physics, see *Blazing Splendor: The Memoirs of Tulku Urgyen Rinpoche* (Boudanath, Nepal: Ranjung Yeshe Publications, 2005).

5. Lochen Dharma Shri, *Releasing Oneself from Essential Delusion—Notes on the Written Instruction in the Vajrasattva Mind Accomplishment of Dreams,* in Gyatrul Rinpoche, *Meditation, Transformation, and Dream Yoga,* trans. B. Alan Wallace and Sangye Khandro (Ithaca, N.Y.: Snow Lion Publications, 2002).

6. This is a practice that is sometimes used in the Tibetan tradition, a buddy system where a companion will, late in the night, whisper in your ear through a rolled-up tube of paper, "This is a dream." Stephen LaBerge has developed a technical aid to achieving lucidity called the *Nova Dreamer.* This masklike device can detect when one is in REM sleep and then emits sounds or light that alert the dreamer that he or she is dreaming.

7. Quoted from the *Dona Sutta: With Dona* (AN 4.36), translated from the Pali by Thanissaro Bhikkhu. *Access to Insight,* 3 July 2010.

8. In the practice of illusory body, all appearances, not just those of the physical body, are regarded as illusions. For an introduction to this practice, see *Natural Liberation.*

Chapter 7. Nighttime Dream Yoga

1. Divine pride means to maintain the sense that one actually is the deity and possesses all of the enlightened qualities of the deity. Confidence in this identity frees one from the limitations of our mundane sense of self. This goes beyond a mere masquerade because eventually one will acquire the qualities of the deity and the meaning of deity practice will become clear.

2. For a detailed explanation of the Tibetan Buddhist mandala, see Denise Patry Leidy and Robert Thurman's

Mandala: The Architecture of Enlightenment (New York: The Overlook Press, 2006).

3. *Introduction to Tantra: The Transformation of Desire,* by Lama Thubten Yeshe (Boston: Wisdom Publications, 2001), is an excellent introduction to deity practice. See also Gyatrul Rinpoche, *The Generation Stage in Buddhist Tantra,* trans. Sangye Khandro (Ithaca, N.Y.: Snow Lion Publications, 2005).

4. This is a mantra often used for purification that can be found in many texts available on Tibetan Buddhism.

5. An offering ritual for purifying negative karma.

6. Lama Jey Tsongkhapa, *A Practice Manual on the Six Yogas of Naropa: Taking the Practice in Hand,* in *Readings on the Six Yogas of Naropa,* ed. G. H. Mullin (Ithaca, N.Y.: Snow Lion Publications, 1997), 97.

7. *Vipashyana* (Sanskrit) is the practice of contemplative insight into fundamental aspects of reality, including the emptiness of inherent nature of all phenomena.

8. *Trekchö* (Tibetan for "cutting through solidity") is the first of the two stages of Dzogchen, designed to break through the substrate consciousness to a direct realization of pristine awareness, which is synonymous with one's own buddha-nature.

9. *Wellsprings of the Great Perfection: The Lives and Insights of the Early Masters,* trans. Erik Pema Kunsang (Kathmandu: Rangjung Yeshe Publications, 2006), 335–36.

10. Jetsunma Tenzin Palmo is now the director of the Dongyu Gatsal Ling nunnery in northern India and is known widely due to Vicki Mackenzie's biography *Cave in the Snow: Tenzin Palmo's Quest for Enlightenment* (New York: Bloomsbury, 1998).

CHAPTER 8. PUTTING YOUR DREAMS TO WORK

1. Arthur Rubinstein, *My Young Years* (New York: Knopf, 1973).

Chapter 9. Individualized Practice and Infrequently Asked Questions

1. The practice of wishing that all sentient beings have happiness, be free from suffering, never be separated from the happiness free of suffering (joy), and that they abide in equanimity. See B. Alan Wallace, *The Four Immeasurables: Practices to Open the Heart* (Ithaca, N.Y.: Snow Lion Publications, 2011).

Chapter 10. Dreaming Yourself Awake: A Wider Perspective

1. A twelve-step sequence revealing the mechanics of rebirth in the cycle of existence known as samsara.
2. Ven. Weragoda Sarada Maha Thero, *Treasury of Truth: Illustrated Dhammapada* (Taipei, Taiwan: The Corporate Body of the Buddha Education Foundation, 1993), 61.
3. Düdjom Lingpa, *The Vajra Essence: From the Matrix of Pure Appearances and Primordial Consciousness, a Tantra on the Self-Originating Nature of Existence*, trans. B. Alan Wallace (Alameda, Calif.: Mirror of Wisdom, 2004), 120–21.
4. According to the Theravada school of Buddhism, this is the earliest compilation of the Buddha's teachings existent today.
5. William James, "The Notion of Consciousness," in *The Writings of William James: A Comprehensive Edition*, ed. John J. McDermott (Chicago: University of Chicago Press, 1977).
6. Stephen W. Hawking and Thomas Hertog, "Populating the Landscape: A Top-Down Approach," *Physical Review D* 73, no. 12 (2006): 123527; Martin Bojowald, "Unique or Not Unique?" *Nature* 442 (Aug. 31, 2006): 988–90.
7. Paul C. W. Davies, "An Overview of the Contributions of John Archibald Wheeler," in *Science and Ultimate Reality: Quantum Theory, Cosmology and Complexity*, edited by

John D. Barrow, Paul C. W. Davies, and Charles L. Harper, Jr. (Cambridge: Cambridge University Press, 2004), 10.

8. William James, *Human Immortality: Two Supposed Objections to the Doctrine* (Boston: Houghton, Mifflin and Company, 1898), 12n3, available at www.des.emory.edu/mfp/james.html; cf. William James, *Essays in Religion and Morality* (Cambridge, Mass.: Harvard University Press, 1989), 75–101.

9. James, *Human Immortality*, 18.

10. Andrei Linde, "Inflation, Quantum Cosmology and the Anthropic Principle," in Barrow et al., eds., *Science and Ultimate Reality*, 426–58.

11. Stephen Hawking, "10 Questions for Stephen Hawking," *TIME Magazine*, Monday, Nov. 15, 2010: www.time.com/time/magazine/article/0,9171,2029483,00.html#ixzz14Pqh5jPN.

12. *Catuḥśataka*, vs. 276. See Ruth Sonam, *Yogic Deeds of Bodhisattvas: Gyel-tsap on Āryadeva's Four Hundred*, commentary by Geshe Sonam Rinchen, trans. Ruth Sonam (Ithaca, N.Y.: Snow Lion Publications, 1994), 239–40.

13. William James, *The Will to Believe, and Other Essays in Popular Psychology* (New York: Longmans, Green, and Co., 1898), 96.

Glossary

arhat. "Worthy one," who has attained the highest level of the Theravada and is liberated from the cycle of birth and death.

bodhichitta. In Mahayana Buddhism, the "awakened mind." Relative bodhichitta is the wish to attain enlightenment for the sake of all sentient beings. Absolute bodhichitta is, from the Dzogchen perspective, synonymous with primordial consciousness.

buddha, a. An "awakened one," one released from the cycle of existence (*samsara*), possessing qualities such as omniscience, unlimited compassion, and a full understanding of the true nature of things.

Buddha, the. The historical buddha Shakyamuni (563–483 B.C.E.) who achieved enlightenment under the bodhi tree in Bodh Gaya (present-day India) and taught the Buddhist Dharma for forty-five years.

buddha realm. (syn.: buddhafield) A pure land that was created through the positive aspiration of a buddha while still a bodhisattva (a being on the path of perfect virtues to enlightenment).

calm abiding. See "meditative quiescence."

critical reflective attitude. A questioning or skeptical attitude applied to mental phenomena, in our case especially to those phenomena appearing in dreams.

DILD. Dream-Initiated Lucid Dream. Term invented by Stephen LaBerge to describe lucid dreams often deliberately triggered by dream content.

dream journal. A diary describing the content of one's dreams.

dream sign. A dream phenomenon that conveys to the dreamer, due to prior preparation, the fact that he or she is presently dreaming.

dream yoga. A traditional practice within Tibetan Buddhism where dreams are used as a path to spiritual awakening.

dullness, laxity. A state where one's attention is unfocused, hazy, and tending to drowsiness.

emptiness. The lack of inherent existence both of phenomena and of the intrinsic duality between subject and object.

enlightenment. Complete awakening, said to include knowledge of all reality in both breadth and depth and an all-embracing compassion, a profound love for all beings.

excitation. Here refers to mental agitation.

ghatika. Sanskrit term for a meditation period of twenty-four minutes, in ancient India said to be the ideal length for beginning meditation training.

hypnagogic imagery. Vivid, dreamlike mental appearances that usually appear prior to dreaming.

illusory body. The practice of viewing all phenomena, including oneself, to be appearing like illusions, like a dream. To view one's body as simply a matrix of illusions.

introspection. In the practice of meditative quiescence, this is a form of quality control where one is continuously aware of the status of one's attention. A type of metacognition that makes one aware of one's degree of mindfulness.

karma. (Sanskrit for "action") According to traditional Buddhist beliefs, one's acts are imprinted in the substrate consciousness (*alaya vijñana*), and the results of those acts (their karma) later come to fruition.

lucid dreaming. Being conscious that you are dreaming while experiencing the dreams of sleep.

meditative quiescence. (Sanskrit: *shamatha*) A group of related meditation techniques that lead to mental stillness.

MILD. Mnemonic Induction of Lucid Dreams. A term invented by Stephen LaBerge for mnemonic devices of prospective memory used to trigger lucidity while dreaming. A dream sign is one example.

mindfulness. Continuous attention to a chosen object, which requires that one remember what the task is and not become distracted by other phenomena.

nyam. (Tibetan for "meditation experience") An anomalous, transient psychological or somatic experience that is catalyzed by proper meditation.

one-pointedness. (Sanskrit: *samadhi*) Perfected meditative concentration where observer and observed are nondual.

Pali Canon. According to the Theravada school of Buddhism, this is the earliest compilation of the Buddha's teachings existent today.

prana. A form of vital energy, in traditional Indian yoga associated with the breath.

primordial consciousness. The deepest and most fundamental level of the mind. A synonym for buddha-nature, absolute bodhichitta, rigpa, darmakaya, pristine awareness, enlightenment.

prospective memory. Here refers to preparing to remember something in a future dream.

psyche. Our ordinary, conditioned mind, comprising the five physical senses along with conscious and unconscious mental phenomena—thoughts, feelings, sensations, and so forth.

quantum physics. Branch of physics originated c. 1900 by Max Planck. Still a foundation of modern physics, quantum physics casts doubt on the materialist basis of traditional Newtonian physics, instead asserting that the building blocks of the universe are nebulous and indeterminate in nature.

relaxation. Here an antidote to agitation.

retrospective memory. Here refers to remembering sequences of dream events from the past.

samadhi. See "one-pointedness."

samaya. A vow or tantric pledge usually given by a teacher when you receive a tantric empowerment.

samsara. In the simplest terms, a dreamlike experience of life after life, propelled by ignorance.

sentient being. Refers generally to unenlightened beings possessing minds and who therefore are capable of thinking, feeling, and perceiving.

settling the body in its natural state. Progressive relaxation of the body allowing it to attain the three qualities of relaxation, stillness, and vigilance.

settling the mind in its natural state. The meditative practice of attention to mental phenomena wherein one observes all appearing mental events—thoughts, mental images, and emotions—neutrally, objectively, without any involvement.

shamatha. See "meditative quiescence."

shavasana. (Sanskrit for "corpse pose") Yogic pose in the supine position.

stillness. Here an antidote to agitation.

substrate. (Sanskrit: *alaya*) The space of the mind that appears to the substrate consciousness: a luminous vacuity in which self, others, and objects disappear.

substrate consciousness. (Sanskrit: *alaya vijñana*) The ground of the ordinary mind, a continuum that persists from life to life and from which springs all ordinary mental activity. Prior to and more fundamental than the subconscious, it is considered the source of the psyche.

twelve links of dependent origination, the. A twelve-step sequence revealing the mechanics of rebirth in the cycle of existence known as *samsara*.

vigilance. Here a mental attitude that counteracts dullness.

WILD. Wake-Initiated Lucid Dreams. A term invented by Stephen LaBerge for the practice of entering into dreams consciously.

working hypothesis. A theory that one tests against experimental evidence or experience in an objective, open-minded way.

Selected Bibliography

His Holiness the Dalai Lama. *Sleeping, Dreaming, and Dying: An Exploration of Consciousness.* Edited by Francisco Varela. Boston: Wisdom Publications, 2002.

———, *Stages of Meditation.* Ithaca, N.Y.: Snow Lion Publications, 2001.

Gyatrul Rinpoche. *Meditation, Transformation, and Dream Yoga.* Translated by B. Alan Wallace and Sangye Khandro. Ithaca, N.Y.: Snow Lion Publications, 2002.

LaBerge, Stephen, and Howard Rheingold. *Exploring the World of Lucid Dreaming.* New York: Ballantine Books, 1990.

———. *Lucid Dreaming.* New York: Random House, 1990.

———. *Lucid Dreaming: A Concise Guide to Awakening in Your Dreams and in Your Life.* Boulder, Colo.: Sounds True, Inc., 2009.

Lamrimpa, Gen. *Calming the Mind.* Ithaca, N.Y.: Snow Lion Publications, 1992.

———. *Realizing Emptiness: Madhyamaka Insight Meditation.* Ithaca, N.Y.: Snow Lion Publications, 1999.

Norbu, Namkai. *The Cycle of Day and Night.* Barrytown, N.Y.: Station Hill Press, 2000.

———. *Dream Yoga and the Practice of Natural Light.* Ithaca, N.Y.: Snow Lion Publications, 2002.

Padmasambhava. *Natural Liberation: Padmasambhava's Teachings on the Six Bardos.* Commentary by Gyatrul Rinpoche, translated by B. Alan Wallace. Boston: Wisdom Publications, 2008.

————. *The Tibetan Book of the Dead*. Translation and commentary by Francesca Fremantle and Chögyam Trungpa. Boston: Shambhala Publications, 1987.

Tenzin Wangyal Rinpoche and Mark Dahlby. *The Tibetan Yogas of Dream and Sleep*. Ithaca, N.Y.: Snow Lion Publications, 1998.

Tsongkhapa, Lama Jey. *A Practice Manual on the Six Yogas of Naropa: Taking the Practice in Hand*. In *Readings on the Six Yogas of Naropa*, edited by G. H. Mullin, 93–135. Ithaca, N.Y.: Snow Lion Publications, 1997.

Urgyen, Tulku. *Blazing Splendor: The Memoirs of Tulku Urgyen Rinpoche*. Boudanath, Nepal: Rangjung Yeshe Publications, 2005.

Wallace, B. Alan. *The Attention Revolution: Unlocking the Power of the Focused Mind*. Boston: Wisdom Publications, 2006.

————. *Genuine Happiness: Meditation as a Path to Fulfillment*. Hoboken, N.J.: John Wiley & Sons, 2005.

————. *Meditations of a Buddhist Skeptic: A Manifesto for the Mind Sciences and Contemplative Practice*. New York: Columbia University Press, 2011.

————. *Mind in the Balance: Meditation in Science, Buddhism, and Christianity*. New York: Columbia University Press, 2009.

————. *The Taboo of Subjectivity: Toward a New Science of Consciousness*. New York: Oxford University Press, 2000.

Index

agitation, 13
amnesia, 26–27
anomalies, 29
atonia, 23
attention
  stabilizing, 1–2, 10–12, 14
  vividness of, 13–16
Attention Revolution: Unlocking the Power of the Focused Mind, The (Wallace), 6
attentional balance (stage of shamatha), 5
"awake," meaning of, 68–69. *See also* waking reality
awakening, spiritual, ix. *See also* enlightenment
awareness
  awareness of, 6, 59–60
  pristine, 59, 92, 93, 107, 108, 147

bardo, 58
bodhichitta, 73, 76–77, 95–97

body
  self and, 82–83
  settling in its natural state, 7
breathing, 7
  mindfulness of, 5–6
  settling it in its natural rhythm, 7, 10, 14, 36–37, 59
breaths, counting twenty-one, 50
Browne, Sir Thomas, x
Buddha (Siddhartha Gautama), 134, 137, 149, 150
  on being awake, 92
  enlightenment, 137, 148
  on mind, 89
  pragmatism, empiricism, and, 69, 77, 149
  on samsara, 137
  on suffering, 73
buddhahood, 69, 73, 95, 97. *See also* enlightenment
Buddhism
  as an empirical tradition, 69

on dream state, 68–69
See also specific topics

Castaneda, Carlos, x
Chagdud Tulku Rinpoche, 87
choiceless awareness, 107
close attention (stage of shamatha), 4
cognizance, 129–30
consciousness
continuity of, 146–50
theories of the origins of,
144, 147
there is no universe without, 143–46
See also dream consciousness; primordial con-
sciousness; substrate
consciousness
continuous attention (stage of
shamatha), 4
counting, 12
creativity, 120–21
critical reflective attitude. *See*
reflective attitude

Dalai Lama, Fourteenth
(Tenzin Gyatso), 77, 97, 110
daydreaming and dreaming,
130
death, 58
deities and deity practice,
97–101, 103
delusion, process of, 85–87,
135–38

Dharma, 78, 124, 148, 150
directed attention (stage of
shamatha), 4
distractions, 13. *See also*
obsessive thinking
dream body, 31
giving it a rubdown, 54
special, 110
spinning your, 54
dream consciousness, 23–26
Dream-Initiated Lucid
Dreams (DILDs), 30, 129
dream lab, 61–62
dream origins, 131–32
dream practice
how to develop an overall
practice, 124–25
individualized practice,
xiv–xv
reviving a dream if your
dream persona is disem-
bodied, 127–28
vividness vs. stability,
126–27
See also specific topics
dream practice sessions
back-to-back, 133
length of, 8
planning, 124–25
dream signs, 28, 41–43, 127
dream yoga, xii–xiv, 21–22,
67–68, 126
lucid dreaming and, 22
See also specific topics
dream yoga practice, 90–92

core practices of emanation and transformation, 103–5
dreaming
  basics of, 22–23
  sources of, 131–33
dreams
  nature of, 129–30
  remembering, 38–39
  subtle cues in realistic, 127
dualism, 138–40
dullness, 13, 15–16, 26, 29
Dzogchen, 107–8

Einstein, Albert, 61
emotions in dreams, 43
emptiness, 74–75, 80, 82, 98, 99
enlightenment, xii
  Buddhist path to, 71, 73–77
  supports in the quest for, 73–77
  See also awareness: pristine; buddhahood
ethics
  Buddhism and, 76–77
  dream yoga and, 76
  in lucid dreaming, 133–34
existence. See nonexistence

faith, 93
food and meditation, 133
Four Immeasurable Virtues, 76
Four Noble Truths, 73, 137, 148
Freud, Sigmund, 70, 119

fully pacified attention (stage of shamatha), 5
fun, 116–17

Gen Lamrimpa, 96
grasping, 86
Gyatrul Rinpoche, xiii, 104

happiness, genuine, ix, 124
Hawking, Stephen, 140–42, 146
healing, psychological and physical, 117–20
Heisenberg, Werner, 83

"I am dreaming," 30, 55–56, 92
illusion, 91. See also delusion
illusory body, practice of, 88–90
insight(s), 56–57, 129–30
intention, 8, 9
interdependence, 81
intuition, 93

James, William, 139, 144–45, 150
Jigme Lingpa, 108
journal, dream, 28, 41–43, 125–26
  purposes of, 28
Jung, Carl Gustav, 70, 117, 118

karma, 71
  as basis of dreams, 132–33

LaBerge, Stephen, xi–xii
  on DILDs, 30
  on dream consciousness
    and waking conscious-
    ness, 90
  on dreams and dreaming,
    23, 25
  *Exploring the World of Lucid
    Dreaming*, 116, 117, 121
  lucid dream research and,
    xi, 119–20
  lucid dreams of, xi, 118
  on MILD, 29, 45
  proof of lucid dreaming,
    19, 21–22
  on wish fulfillment, 116
laxity, 11, 15–17
letting go, 7–8, 37
Linde, Andrei, 146
Longchen Rabjam
    (Longchenpa), 108
lucid dreaming, x–xii
  balancing dream yoga and,
    xiv
  complementary strategies
    for, 46–48
  defined, x
  getting started with, 37–40
  motivation for, 27–31, 38
  strategies for increasing the
    chances of, 27–31
  training in, 31–32
lucid-dreaming techniques,
    34. *See also specific
    techniques*

lucid dream(s)
  anticipating, 27
  concentrating focus on an
    object within a, 54
  creating stories and conti-
    nuity within, 57
  extending your, 53
  "flat," 126
  keeping the dream alive,
    53–55
  putting them to use, 32–34
  source of teachings re-
    ceived in, 134
lucidity
  directly cultivating, 48–49
  intensity of dreams and,
    129–30
  keeping it alive, 55–56
  strategies for, 26–27
  using anticipation con-
    sciously to maintain, 57
luminosity, types of, 129–30

meditation
  a space for, 62
  stages of, 3–5
meditation session for settling
    the mind in its natural
    state, 49–51
memory
  prospective, 2, 27–28, 39, 100
  retrospective, 2, 38
mental images, releasing, 37
mind
  quieting the, 8, 37

settling it in its natural
  state, 48–51
mind wandering, 136, 146. *See
  also* obsessive thinking
mindfulness
  defined, 9
  enhancing and developing
    the faculty of, 15
Mlodinow, Leonard, 142
Mnemonic Induction of
  Lucid Dreams (MILD),
  29, 45, 46
motivation, power of, 27–31

*Natural Liberation: Padma-
  sambhava's Teachings on
  the Six Bardos*, 80, 107.
  See also Padmasambhava
Nicklaus, Jack, 120
nightmares, 9, 56, 104–6, 117, 132
nighttime dream yoga
  hindrances, 101–3
  motivation for, 95–97
nighttime dream yoga
  practice, 97–98
nonexistence, 80–85, 87, 90,
  98. *See also* delusion;
  illusory body
nothingness, 74, 80
NREM (non-rapid eye move-
  ment) sleep, 22–23, 48
nyam, 105

object and subject, emergence
  of, 138–40

objects in dreams, 43
  concentrating focus on, 54
obsessive thinking, 11–12,
  100, 136. *See also* mind
  wandering
open presence, 58–59, 107–8

pacified attention (stage of
  shamatha), 5
Padmasambhava, 88, 95, 98,
  106
  on the dream state, 103,
    105, 107
  dream yoga teachings,
    79–85, 90–93, 103
  instructions for falling
    asleep, 99
  *Natural Liberation: Padma-
    sambhava's Teachings on
    the Six Bardos*, 80, 107
  on nonexistence, 80–83, 85
  visualizing him at your
    throat chakra, 99
paranormal experiences and
  abilities, 108–10
people in dreams, 43
Pepys, Samuel, x
performance training, 120–21
personal deities, 97–99, 103
phenomena, 81, 85
  mind precedes, 89
  See also nonexistence
physics, modern, 84
  mind and matter in, 140–46
positive attitude, 7, 40

posture, comfortable, 7,
    49–50, 59
pragmatism, 77–78
prana, 110
primordial consciousness,
    70–73, 92–93
    breaking through to, 107–11
prospective memory, 2, 27–28,
    39, 100
psyche, xii–xiii, 117, 118, 131
    defined, 70
psychology, 21, 70
purification, lucid dreaming
    and, 129

qualia, 73
quantum physics. *See* physics

"reality," 85, 90
    understanding, 87
    See also nonexistence
recurrent dream signs, 127.
    See also dream signs
reflective attitude, critical, 29
    developing a, 29–30, 43–44
relaxation, 6–9, 11, 13
REM (rapid eye movement)
    sleep, 22–23
resurgent attention (stage of
    shamatha), 4
retrospective memory, 2, 38
Rubinstein, Arthur, 120

samadhi, 4–5, 63, 95, 106, 109, 110

samsara, xii, xiii, 73, 90,
    136–38, 149, 150
self, personal, 82–83
shadow, 117
shamatha, xiv, 1–2, 5, 99,
    130
    basic technique of, 9
    dream yoga and, 78, 102–3
    Padmasambhava and, 103
    in practice, 6–12
    ten stages in the develop-
        ment of, 4–5
    in theory, 3–5
    three sequential practices
        on the path of, 5–6
    training in, 2–4, 55
    without a sign, 6, 59–60
    See also specific topics
shamatha practices, 107
    to improve sleep, 36–37
single-pointed attention
    (stage of shamatha), 5
Six Perfections, 76
sleep
    basics of, 22–23
    lucid dreamless, 57–59
    shamatha practice to
        improve, 36–37
sleep problems, 35
"sorcerer phase" of dream
    yoga, 103
Stages of Meditation
    (Kamalashila), 3
state checks, 28, 44, 53

daytime, 44–46
stillness, 13. *See also* waking:
    remaining immobile
    upon
strange loop, 142, 143
subject and object, emergence
    of, 138–40
substrate consciousness, xiii,
    70–73
    dream yoga and, 72
    suffering, 73

tactile field of the body, filling
    the, 14
tactile sensations, letting
    awareness permeate the
    field of, 10, 50
tamed attention (stage of
    shamatha), 4
Ten Non-virtues, 76
Tenzin Palmo, 108
"This is a dream," 55–56, 90, 93
thoughts, letting go of, 8, 37
Tibetan Buddhism, 74–78.
    See also specific topics

transformation
    practice of, 103–4
    semilucid, 128

understanding reality, 87

Varela, Francisco, 130
vigilance, 13

Wake-Initiated Lucid Dreams
    (WILDs), 31, 46–48
waking, remaining immobile
    upon, 38–39
waking consciousness, 24
    dream consciousness and,
    25, 90, 101
waking reality, dreaming,
    and illusion, 85, 86,
    88, 91–93, 143. *See also*
    "awake"; nonexistence
Wheeler, John, 142, 143

yidam, 97

Zong Rinpoche, xiii